How to Be a
SECTOR
INVESTOR

Other Books in the McGraw-Hill Mastering the Market Series

How to Be a Value Investor, Lisa Holton, ISBN: 0-07-079401-4

How to Be a Small-Cap Investor, David Newton, ISBN: 0-07-047183-5

How to Be a Growth Investor, Valerie F. Malter and Stuart P. Kaye, ISBN: 0-07-040068-7

Essential Guides to Today's Most Popular Investment Strategies

How to Be a
SECTOR
INVESTOR

DR. LARRY HUNGERFORD
STEVE HUNGERFORD

McGraw-Hill

New York San Francisco Washington, D.C. Auckland Bogotá
Caracas Lisbon London Madrid Mexico City Milan
Montreal New Delhi San Juan Singapore
Sydney Tokyo Toronto

Library of Congress Cataloging-in-Publication Data

Hungerford, Larry.
How to be a sector investor
/ by Larry Hungerford and Steve Hungerford.
p. cm.—(McGraw-Hill mastering the market series)
ISBN 0-07-134522-1
1. Portfolio management. I. Hungerford, Steve. II. Title.
III. Series.
HG4529.5.H86 1999
332.6—dc21 99-15643
CIP

McGraw-Hill

A Division of The *McGraw-Hill* Companies

1 2 3 4 5 6 7 8 9 0   AGM/AGM   9 0 9 8 7 6 5 4 3 2 1 0 9

ISBN 0-07-134522-1

*The sponsoring editor for this book was Roger Marsh, the editing supervisor
was Donna Muscatello, and the production supervisor was Elizabeth J. Strange.
It was set in Times Roman per the MMS design by Joanne Morbit of McGraw-
Hill's Professional Book Group composition unit.*

Printed and bound by Arcata Graphics.

This publication is designed to provide accurate and authoritative information
in regard to the subject matter covered. It is sold with the understanding that
neither the author nor the publisher is engaged in rendering legal, accounting,
or other professional services. If legal advice or other expert assistance is
required, the services of a competent professional person should be sought.

> *—From a Declaration of Principles jointly adopted by a Committee
> of the American Bar Association and a Committee of Publishers.*

CONTENTS

Part Three: Putting It All Together

FOREWORD

There is much more to sector investing than simply understanding what comprises a sector. Professional investors often use economic data ranging from gross domestic product (GDP) to inflation and interest rates to help them determine which sectors offer the best risk/reward opportunity. For example, rising interest rates generally deter purchases of durable consumer goods like automobiles or washers. People are not as likely to finance big-ticket items if higher rates cause monthly payments to balloon. In this scenario, it would be prudent to avoid buying durable goods stocks. So then, individuals interested in sector investing should have a basic understanding of economics aided by some knowledge of stock analysis. But too often individuals will follow the crowd as they chase the latest and hottest sector. Speculating without knowledge is a recipe for disaster. Luck should not be confused with knowledge. A superficial understanding of a subject is not the same as doing your homework. And playing a hunch is often worse than no understanding at all. That being said, this book should start the investor toward a basic understanding of investing in the various sectors. Its intent is not to give you an in-depth knowledge of sector analysis. That would entail several volumes. Rather, the following pages should simply get you started.

Dr. Larry Hungerford and I have worked together for more than seven years. He performs fund analysis and helps shape investment policy for our firm. He has always been fascinated by the unusual investment opportunity, whether a remote foreign country or a unique domestic business.

Larry quite often explores away from the more traditional mainstream investments, looking at the less obvious. These areas require more knowledge and more work, but may reward investors well, or punish them. Reading about investments is not only Larry's vocation, but his hobby as well. He voraciously consumes journal after journal, digesting the analysis of many financial experts. Dr. Hungerford and his son Steve are well known locally for helping individual investors "do it themselves" using no-load mutual funds. They believe that most individuals, with patience and hard work, can be good investors. Their initial advice is typically:

1. Start early (when you are young).
2. Pay yourself first (put money in your retirement plan).
3. Diversify (you can't know the future).

Sector investing is a critical component to managing your investing portfolio, and a thorough understanding of sector investing can contribute to overall portfolio performance. If a particular sector looks weak, you certainly would think twice about a short-term commitment. However, short-term weakness may create a buying opportunity for long-term investment. A good knowledge of the various sectors may prompt investing in a temporarily beleaguered sector, through either a diversified mutual fund or individual stocks. Or a proper understanding may well prevent investing in a weak sector just before it weakens further. Regardless, always remember what your mother told you about the danger of putting all your eggs in one basket. Then again, you might want to tell her what it is like to pick just the right basket (or sector).

John B. Woodard
Woodard & Company Asset Management Group, Inc.
Winston-Salem, NC

PREFACE

Why would anyone pick up a book on sector investing? More specifically, why would you pick up a book on sector investing? Our guess is: *profit*! You want your investments to make more money. You are not satisfied with just getting to first base—you want to swing hard for doubles, triples, and even home runs. Let's face it: you are a capitalist to the core, and perhaps a bit greedy. You have seen some of the eye-popping numbers that certain sector mutual funds have produced over the years. You want a piece of the action. Nothing wrong with that. Indeed, we admire your aggressiveness.

But lurking just beyond the recesses of your capitalist greed lies an even more destructive force. It is an emotion that makes you hesitate, that calls you to inaction, and that constantly reminds you of every investing horror story you've ever heard. That emotion: fear. Fear is, in our opinion, the more dangerous of the two emotions that plague most investors.

The desire for profit encourages us to invest in the stock market, rather than leave our savings tucked safely away in low-yielding investments. Capitalist greed compels us to take risk, to seek ownership, and to share in the profits of the great businesses of the world. Given enough time and proper diversification, investing in the more volatile arena of stocks is always the right thing to do. (It is short-term greed that usually causes the big problems.)

Fear, on the other hand, cripples the average investor and leads to inaction. Fear often causes large sums of money to languish in money markets or CDs. As a result, real returns, after taxes, barely keep up with inflation. Or fear may lead to far too much invested in corporate or government bonds. Either way, you lose the energizing power of double-digit annual compounding that stocks have produced decade after decade. (U.S. stocks have averaged 9.1% for 128 years since 1871 and 12.2% for the 50-plus years since World War II.)

So ask yourself: are you ready to face your fear, push past anxiety, and embrace the possibility of sector investing? Are you willing to risk a few strikeouts along the way as you swing for the fences? Conversely, are you interested in diversifying part of your portfolio into real estate, utilities, and natural resources—sectors that often zig when the broad market zags? If so, we invite you to join us as we journey together down the path of intelligent, risk/reward sector investing.

In the following pages we hope to answer most of the questions that you, as a beginning or intermediate investor, want answered. We make no apologies to the advanced or professional investor; this book is not written for you. We opt for a fairly basic approach, assuming no prior knowledge of sector investing or complicated terminology.

Part One (Chapters 1 through 3) will help you get started. In Chapter 1 we explain what sector investing means, define key terms, and provide a framework for you to build a personal basic investing philosophy. Though many professionals don't include international investing as a specific sector, we explain why we do. Chapters 2 and 3 describe the pathways to investing in various sectors—using mutual funds and/or buying individual stocks—with emphasis on the practical steps of each method. Part Two (Chapters 4 through 10) provides you with a complete toolbox for sector investing. Here we devote a separate chapter to each of our chosen sectors, with an interview and advice from a successful mutual fund manager in that sector. Part Three (Chapters 11 and 12) is designed to help you put it all together. In Chapter 11 we offer model portfolios together with a step-by-step approach to getting started, complete with phone numbers and references. Chapter 12 concludes with a few cautions and warnings (fear is sometimes a good thing).

In this book, we feature the seven major sectors of the stock market as we see them. These sectors can be divided into two major groups. The first group consists of those sectors that generally move in concert with

U.S. stocks. This group includes technology and communications, financial services, health care, and international investing. All four of these sectors are more likely to move in the same direction as the broad U.S. stock market, though certainly less so in the international arena. The second group of sectors is much like a band of wayward adolescents: they have to find their own direction. These sectors sometimes are up when the broader markets decline and often are down when other stocks move higher. They include utilities, real estate, and natural resources.

A different division of sectors or subsectors may seem more logical or appropriate to your particular investment objectives. We have chosen what we feel are the largest segments of the market and believe the principles outlined can be applied to other U.S. sectors and subsectors, as well as to segments of the international arena, such as emerging markets.

After reading the first three chapters, you may want to skip to the sectors that have the most appeal to you. Although we believe there are valuable investment tips in each sector chapter and from each expert interview, you may find reading selected chapters a more efficient use of your time. Whatever you do, we ask that you please read the last two chapters carefully. They contain our blueprint for sector investing and, perhaps more important, offer a warning against too much greed with a stark example of the pitfalls inherent in sector investing.

As you pick the sectors that appeal to you, we hope that our approach will help you secure higher returns or greater diversification to lower risk—or both. Simply put: our overall goal in this book is to help you discover your sector investment comfort level—balancing both fear and greed.

Larry Hungerford
Steve Hungerford

ACKNOWLEDGMENTS

Special thanks to:

John and Joan Woodard, for being such understanding colleagues and friends, and for answering seemingly endless questions.

Jennifer Angell, for picking up the slack in the office.

Sue Hungerford, for being such a supportive wife.

All the mutual fund managers who agreed to be interviewed. Without you, this book would not have been possible.

Getting Started

CHAPTER 1

What's a Sector?
Why Invest?

$\int$ ectors, sectors, sectors....What are they and why would anyone
choose to invest in them? This is, after all the central question we hope
to answer here. Essentially, the "why" of sector investing comes down
to the potential for huge gains, or as we stated in the Preface: it's about the
possibility of watching one's portfolio value soar. In short, the "why" is
about making more money. There is, of course, also the potential for economic disaster. Out-of-favor sectors can plunge even as the broad market
is posting nice gains. It becomes gut wrenching to watch hard-earned savings dwindle as once highly favored sectors lose their market appeal. So
sector investing is the classic trade-off: the old story of higher risk producing either bigger gains or larger losses. That's the fun, or maybe the
horror, of sector investing. With that said, let us begin.

Sector Defined

What exactly is a sector? Briefly stated, a sector is a segment, a part of
the whole. A sector of the stock market is simply a part or segment of the

overall stock market—a niche in the economy. Market sectors are made up of groups of stocks that represent certain industries. The *Wall Street Journal* each day lists the performance of 77 Dow Jones Global Industry Groups for four areas of the world—the United States, the Americas (including the United States), Europe, and Asia/Pacific. When bundled together, kindred industry groups are classified into market sectors. For instance, the *Journal*'s technology sector includes stocks from the following nine industrial groups:

Aerospace/defense	Medical/biotech
Communications technology	Office equipment
Computers	Semiconductors
Diversified technology	Software
Industrial technology	

In other words, the technology sector includes companies that manufacture every technological device imaginable from cell phones to ZIP drives, software to sophisticated medical equipment, as well as those companies that offer technological services, such as the Internet providers. Other sectors can be much simpler. For example, the Dow Jones utilities sector has only four industry groups: electric, gas, telephone, and water.

Morningstar, Inc. (the leading mutual fund research and rating company, located in Chicago) generally tracks 10 sectors in the research that it provides. They are:

Consumer durables	Industrial cyclicals
Consumer staples	Retail
Energy	Services
Financial	Technology
Health care	Utilities

Of these 10, we will be specifically addressing the five in this book that historically have been of most interest to purchasers of U.S. stocks. Three are currently the big favorites of most investors: financial services, health care, and technology (including global communications). The other two traditional sectors are utilities (often favored by older investors) and natural resources, where we focus on energy, but also include hard assets, such as gold, silver, and other commodities.

RESEARCH TIP

Every day *Investor's Business Daily* ranks 197 industry groups on price performance of all stocks in the industry during the latest six-month period. Cost: $1.

Another increasingly popular sector that has blossomed in the 1990s is commercial real estate. Stung by limited partnership fiascoes in the early 1980s and ever more restrictive lending policies of banks during the past decade, big-time commercial landlords have gone public to raise huge amounts of capital to develop and purchase property. They have created nearly $500 billion worth of real estate investment trusts (REITs) that trade daily on the stock exchanges and offer yearly dividend yields that average nearly 7%.

Our seventh and final sector, international investing, is technically *not* a sector at all, even though CNBC and other financial media often include it in their reports on sector performance. Actually, buying stocks of corporations based in foreign countries, or "international sector" investing, is usually defined as investing in an asset class, like buying small-company stocks or buying bonds. While we recognize that internationals are *not* a sector in the strictest definition of the word, they nonetheless represent a huge segment of the investing universe. We include such investment here for several reasons: (1) internationals are an important component of a diversified portfolio; (2) about half the world's stock market wealth is located outside the United States; and (3) beginning investors often shy away from international investing simply from a lack of understanding.

Contributing to the negligible role for international stocks in most portfolios has been the sensational returns for U.S. stocks during the 1990s compared with their foreign counterparts. Many investors look at recent U.S. stock returns and think, "Who needs international stocks!"

But even though U.S. stock averages have beaten foreign stock averages over the last five years (1994–1998), just six years ago, in 1993, the average U.S. stock mutual fund returned 13%, while the average international fund jumped 38%, and the average emerging-markets fund soared 66%. (See Table 1-1 and Figure 1-1.) Also, for two decades prior to the 1990s, international stocks, as represented by Europe, Australia, and the Far East (the EAFE index), increased nearly 11 times (1,096%), while the average return for U.S. stocks, as represented by the S&P 500 stock index, rose just over 7 times (709%). (See Figure 1-2.) Further, the results from investing internationally can be incredibly diverse. For

TABLE 1-1   United States Versus Internationals, 1994–1998

Year	S&P 500 Index	Morningstar's Foreign Stock Average
1994	1.31%	1.80%
1995	37.53%	6.86%
1996	22.95%	12.90%
1997	33.35%	6.05%
1998	28.58%	8.53%

Data Source: Morningstar, Inc.

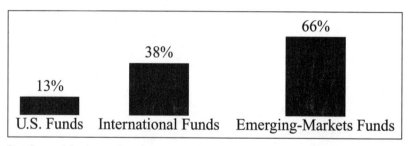

Data Source: Morningstar, Inc.

FIGURE 1-1   United States Versus Internationals, 1993 Fund Averages

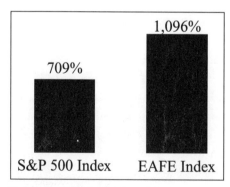

Data Source: Morningstar, Inc.

FIGURE 1-2   United States Versus Internationals, 1970–1989

example, European mutual funds gained 20% annually for the three years from 1996 to 1998, while Asian Pacific funds lost 11% annually during the same period.

Further confusion results from international investing's many specialized segments. Knowledgeable investors often speak of the differences between "developed" foreign countries (Western Europe, Canada, Japan, Australia, and New Zealand) and "emerging markets" (Africa, Eastern Europe, India, Latin America, and most Pacific Rim countries). In addition, each individual country, with its unique economic issues and government policies, can be considered a subsector of the overall international market. In fact, some funds called "closed-end" funds invest in only one particular country. As we write this in early 1999, we personally own three individual closed-end mutual funds that invest in only one country each—Australia, Austria, and Chile. (See Chapter 2 for an explanation of open-end and closed-end mutual funds.)

Obviously, it would be impossible to delve into every imaginable sector and subsector of the market. So, for the purposes of this book, we have narrowed our attention to seven: technology (and global communications), financial services, health care, international, real estate, utilities, and natural resources. We believe these seven to be sufficiently broad and the most critical for the average investor. However, once the principles explored in these next few pages are understood, they can be applied to any market sector or subsector that might be of specific interest to you.

RESEARCH TIP

By far the most timely and comprehensive periodic review of industry groups is Standard and Poor's industry surveys, published each week. Each booklet, typically 30 to 40 pages (very small print), provides comprehensive statistical information on companies in the group and an in-depth analysis of the industry's challenges and prospects. We found the S&P industry surveys at our local library; for subscription information for your library or to purchase a single issue, call 800 221-5277.

Listed below are the 52 S&P industry groups; each is reviewed at least semiannually. Notice that computers are considered so important that they rate five topics. For health care sector aficionados, there are four booklets: (1) facilities, (2) managed care, (3) pharmaceuticals, and (4) products and supplies (as well as a survey on biotechnology).

Aerospace and Defense

Agribusiness

Airlines

Alcoholic Beverages and Tobacco

Apparel and Footwear

Autos and Auto Parts

Banking

Biotechnology

Broadcasting and Cable

Capital Goods

Chemicals: Basic

Chemicals: Specialty

Communications Equipment

Computers: Commercial Services

Computers: Consumer Services and the Internet

Computers: Hardware

Computers: Networking

Computers: Software

Electric Utilities

Environmental and Waste Management

Financial Services: Diversified

Foods and Nonalcoholic Beverages

Health Care: Facilities

Health Care: Managed Care

Health Care: Pharmaceuticals

Health Care: Products and Supplies

Homebuilding

Household Durables

Household Nondurables

Insurance: Life and Health

Insurance: Property-Casualty

Investment Services

Leisure Products

Lodging and Gaming

Metals: Industrial

Metals: Precious

Movies and Home Entertainment

Natural Gas Distribution

Oil and Gas: Equipment and Services

Oil and Gas: Production and Marketing

Paper and Forest Products

Publishing

Restaurants

Retailing: General

Retailing: Specialty

Savings and Loans

Semiconductor Equipment

Semiconductors

Supermarkets and Drugstores

Telecommunications: Wireless

Telecommunications: Wireline

Transportation: Commercial

A Philosophy for Sector Investing

Why become a sector investor? Why not stick to plain vanilla-flavored investing? You could simply follow the standard conservative advice and stick 70% of your money in large-company U.S. stocks and 30% in high-quality bonds. Then again, if simplicity were the fountain from which you wished to drink, you would not be reading this book. You are undoubtedly willing to swallow a little complexity in your search for higher returns.

So then, what role should sector investing play in your overall portfolio? This is the critical first decision, and only you can make it, though we willingly offer our suggestions. First of all, diversification is the key tenet to all long-term investing. By diversification, we mean allocating certain percentages of your investments to core asset classes. To our way of thinking, these broad asset classes number five: large-cap stocks, mid-cap stocks, small-cap stocks, international stocks, and for older or more conservative investors, bonds.

To define small, mid-, and large caps, we use the Morningstar definitions of company size. In December 1998, Morningstar instituted a new method for differentiating among large-, mid-, and small-size companies on the basis of the 5,000 largest stocks in its database. Of those 5,000 stocks, the biggest 250 are considered "large cap." The next 750 are labeled "midcap," and the remaining 4,000 are "small cap." As of late 1998, the method rates a company in the United States as "small" if its market capitalization is less than $1.2 billion. Midcaps have a market capitalization between $1.2 and $8.3 billion, and U.S. large caps, according to Morningstar, are companies whose outstanding shares are worth $8.3 billion or more. The Morningstar criteria are the generally accepted industry standard for U.S. stocks and are accepted here as well.

FORMULA

Market capitalization is a term used to measure the total value of all the outstanding shares of a particular company's stock. It's simply the number of shares times the price per share. Its formula is as follows:

Number of Shares Outstanding × Current Price per Share = Market Capitalization

The core asset classes should be the first purchases any investor makes. For most investors, the best, and certainly the easiest, way to invest in these core holdings is through mutual funds. Although it's certainly possible to invest by using individual stocks, mutual funds offer instant diversification within an asset class and can be bought without paying a commission. (See Chapter 2 for our discussion of no-load mutual funds.)

Once core holdings are in place, an investor highly tolerant of volatility may want to seek increased overall portfolio returns by adding the potentially high-octane performance that sectors offer. Pushing the edge of the investing envelope is indeed the goal of sector experimentation. And each year, when all open-end mutual funds are ranked, a sector fund often rates as the number 1 performing fund for the year. Three times in the 1990s, the number 1 fund has more than doubled: biotech in 1991, gold in 1993, and an Internet fund in 1998. Conversely, sector funds also invariably end up dead last on the yearly list of worst funds. Thus, adding the right sectors at the right time can increase an investor's return significantly, while adding the wrong sectors at the wrong time can be disastrous.

Just for your perusal, we list the top-performing leader and worst laggard each year from 1991 to 1998 for open-end mutual funds. Notice that the sensational 265% return for Lexington Strategic Investments (primarily a South African gold fund) in 1993 followed a 61% loss by the same fund in 1992. A 61% loss followed by a 265% gain nets an investor a total two-year gain of 3%! (See Tables 1-2 and 1-3.) Avoiding disaster and enhancing returns by targeting certain sectors is the central reason for writing this book. To accomplish such a goal as a beginning or intermediate investor, you would do well to adopt a 50% rule. Don't invest more than half your portfolio in sector funds. Diversify the other 50% in the

TABLE 1-2   The Yearly Winners

Year	Winner	Change
1991	Oppenheimer Global Biotech	Up 121%
1992	Fidelity Select Savings and Loan	Up 58%
1993	Lexington Strategic Investments	Up 265%
1994	Seligman Communications and Information	Up 35%
1995	Alger Capital Appreciation	Up 79%
1996	State Street Global Research	Up 71%
1997	American Heritage	Up 75%
1998	Internet Fund	Up 196%

Data source: Morningstar, Inc.; *Wall Street Journal.*

TABLE I-3   The Yearly Losers

Year	Loser	Change
1991	Strategic Gold/Minerals	Down 28%
1992	Lexington Strategic Investments	Down 61%
1993	Pilgrim Corporate Utilities	Down 18%
1994	Montrend Gold	Down 50%
1995	Eaton Vance Greater India	Down 33%
1996	Matthews International Korea	Down 32%
1997	Matthews International Korea	Down 65%
1998	Pro Ultra-Short OTC	Down 51%

Data source: Morningstar, Inc.; *Wall Street Journal.*

core asset classes previously discussed. Remember: sector investing increases your risk of losing money. Managing that risk is the subject to which we now turn.

Types of Risk

In the investment arena, **risk** is a term batted about more than a beach ball loose in a packed baseball stadium. Unfortunately, risk is often tougher to corral than a foul ball hit into those same stadium seats. Though many pursue, only one lucky fan comes away with the ball. Risk is much the same. Talked about by many, understood by few.

The core problem is that there are many different types of risk. Inflation risk that eats at purchasing power over time is one type. Interest rate risk that can send bond prices plummeting is another. But when it comes to ownership of common stocks, the three main threats stalking invested cash are business risk, industry risk, and market risk.

Business Risk

Business risk refers to the possibility of a company's stock price declining because of inherent factors attributable to the actions of that particular company. The overriding fear fueling business risk centers on declining profits and even possible bankruptcy. Although an industry,

During the same 10-year period that Brendles went bankrupt (1986–1996), another retailer, Arkansas-based WalMart, more than quadrupled in value.

such as insurance, may be healthy overall, inept management and bad underwriting can lead to declining profits and increased business risk. In a variety of businesses, factors such as a poor product line, lousy marketing, changing consumer preferences, and a sullied reputation can lead to a sea of red ink and a company's eventual failure, leaving the underlying stock virtually worthless.

Brendles is a good example of business risk. Based in North Carolina, Brendles was a discount retailer that began trading as an IPO (initial public offering) at $18 in 1986. We bought the stock a few weeks later at $17, confident we had found a bargain—since the stock was $2 below its peak price of $19. A year later (before the 1987 crash) we sold it at $12 a share, no longer convinced of our bargain. A friend of ours bought it "cheap" a couple of years later at $6 a share, even though we told him: "Steve, that dog won't hunt." He then sold a year later at $5. In 1996, Brendles filed for bankruptcy; its shares became worthless. That's business risk!

Industry Risk

Industry risk is the movement of stock prices in response to trends and investors' perceptions regarding a specific industry. Financial professionals claim that industry risk accounts for at least 50% of an individual stock's price movement—some argue it may be as high as 80%.

A classic example is the effect of oil prices on the airline stocks. Because fuel costs are such a big part of each airline's operating costs, significant daily movements in oil prices generally have an inverse effect on the price of airline stocks. That is, as oil prices go up, airline stock prices go down (and vice versa). Another dramatic example of industry risk is the Clinton administration's attempt to pass federally regulated universal health care in 1993 and early 1994. With the proposed tight controls on drug prices, the whole pharmaceutical industry nose-dived; for example, the market leader Merck, the largest U.S. pharmaceutical company, declined more than 50%. As fears of excessive federal regulation disappeared, the health care sector rallied; by the beginning of 1999, Merck was more than five times higher than its 1994 low.

Market Risk

Market risk, on the other hand, happens along every time some critical world event or new piece of economic information rattles Wall Street. The shock waves are generally felt on stock prices across the board, whether or not a particular individual company has reported bad news. A critical piece of market news could range from higher interest rates to an impending war. Usually a sense of doom and gloom surrounds the professional trader. This is often a good time to buy. As pessimism abounds, stock prices fall and buying opportunities become abundant.

One of these market quakes hit on October 26, 1997. It registered near the top of the metaphorical economic Richter scale. The impetus for this particular quake was the Asian monetary crisis.

The Hong Kong market slid dramatically on fears of an impending devaluation of its local currency, which is linked to the U.S. dollar. European markets quickly sold off to help trigger a one-day S&P 500 decline of 7% as sellers swamped buyers. Anyone who happened to *need* cash on that day quickly understood market risk. The next day, stock prices continued to drop during the first hour of trading before institutional (and individual) investors decided that stocks were selling at bargain rates; buyers then overwhelmed sellers as the overall market rose more than 3%, gaining back almost half its previous day's loss.

Anyone who held on saw the market rise quickly from the financial rubble in October 1997 to set new highs just six months later. And such is the case with market risk. It's generally a relatively short-term phenomenon, unless the economy hits the protracted skids. Serious recessions (or a depression) and/or sharply higher interest rates are almost always the major reasons for "bear" markets, which are typically defined as a 20% or more decline from market highs.

> As bad as the October 26, 1997 sell-off was, it didn't approach either of the two worst one-day market crashes, in October 1987 and October 1929. Both sell-offs were more than twice as bad as the 7% 1997 decline.

A Word About Risk

Everyone hates risk. Whether it's a flight from Denver to Chicago or a drive on the Blue Ridge Parkway in the scenic Appalachians, everyone wants to feel safe. A possible exception are those rare individuals who actually enjoy strapping a little square pack on their back and hurling themselves out of a plane at 2,000 feet. These sky divers and other thrill seekers get a "rush" from their favorite chance-taking activity. Still, most of us try to reduce risk as much as possible. And when it comes to investing, risk reduction is always an important consideration.

But what about risk versus reward? It's obvious that a certain amount of risk is required to make appreciable gains in any portfolio. We quite often meet investors, many of them baby boomers, who, for the past five years, have safely invested in various fixed-income instruments, either money market or guaranteed investment contracts, in their 401(k)s. Avoiding the stock mutual funds in their 401(k)s by making the "safe" decision has cost them huge amounts of money. Certainly their "risk" decision was the wrong one—giving up the opportunity to have their money work as hard for them as they work for their money.

So the crucial question is: how is risk defined? Most investors (and even investment professionals) confuse risk with normal market volatility or fluctuation. Thus, CDs are judged as "safe" because they do not fluctuate in price, and stocks are considered risky because they do. And there's the rub. In most discussions about risk, investment time horizon is totally ignored.

We argue that risk is much more a symptom of investment time horizon than of normal market fluctuations. Let us illustrate. Suppose that Mary, a 42-year-old woman, has $100,000 that she wants to begin using in retirement at age 60. In this hypothetical scenario, we'll give only two alternatives. Option 1 is to play it "safe" and put all her money in CDs paying 6% a year. Option 2 is to take a "risk" and put her money into a large-company U.S. stock fund that manages to yield only a "below average" return of 10% a year, with a couple of great years earning Mary 20% or more and a few other years giving her a loss of 10% to 15%. (From 1871 to 1997, large-company U.S. stocks have had an average annual compound return of 9.1%. Since 1926, the average has been 10.6%, and since World War II, it's been 12.2%.)

Choosing option 1, Mary would have approximately $285,000 when she retired. Under option 2, she would have almost twice as

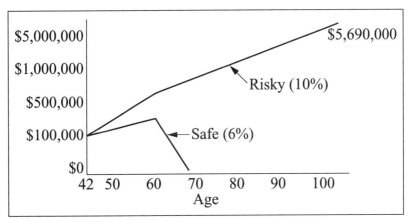

FIGURE 1-3   The Two Choices of Mary Reader: "Safe" Versus "Risky"

much, about $556,000. Now if in retirement she were to need $40,000 a year to live on and were to continue making 6% a year, then under option 1, she would run out of money before age 70, barring any other source of income. Under option 2, where she continues to average 10% annually, she would never run out of money. In fact, her account would actually grow to just about $5,690,000 if she lived to age 100, and with $40,000 withdrawals per year, she would have spent $1,600,000. The main point here is that there is no real danger to investing in a well-diversified basket of stocks, presupposing a long enough time horizon. (See Figure 1-3.)

Even during the worst economic crisis our nation has ever seen—the Great Depression in which the Dow Jones Industrial Average (DJIA) fell from a high of 381 in September 1929 to a low of 41 in July 1932, an 89% decline—even investors who bought at the top in 1929 would have not lost a single dollar if they hadn't sold until 1944 (15 years later). In fact, there has never been a 15-year period in this century where investors would have lost any of their original principal by buying the average-performing U.S. stock. Also, the difference between the value of one dollar invested over 72 years (last day of 1925 to last day of 1997) in long-term government bonds versus large-company U.S. stocks is enormous. According to Ibbotsen Associates, bonds would be worth $39, whereas large-company stocks would equal $1,828. Granted, that's more than a seven-decade time horizon, but certainly stocks are the investment of choice for the average baby boomer (age 42 in 1998) not planning to touch her IRA or 401(k) money until retirement.

So barring some unforeseen cataclysmic event that topples the U.S. government, long-term diversified stock investing is indeed safe. Of course, should an Armageddon-type scenario play itself out in our lifetime, then we are all in serious trouble anyway, whether our money is invested in stocks, bonds, or some FDIC-insured money market fund. The real danger to the long-term investor in efficient markets such as the United States is *not* the up-and-down gyrations of the market over the short term. The real danger for our 60-year-old retiree, Mary, facing "imminent" death at age 100, is the possibility that she will outlive her money. Modern medicine has expanded the human life span. Invest with that in mind, realizing that long-term investing in great businesses of the world is actually a much safer risk/reward choice than fixed-income or bond investments. According to Jeremy Seigel, author of *Stocks for the Long Run* (McGraw-Hill, 1998), there has never been a single 30-year period since the Civil War in which bonds have beaten stocks. Even over all 10-year periods since 1871, stocks win five times out of six. So then, long-term investment choices driven by fear of short-term fluctuations are actually a much higher risk option than a well-diversified stock portfolio.

The Unique Risks of Sector Investing

With that said, sector investing is slightly different from the diversified approach that most financial professionals advocate and that we will be discussing at greater length in the next chapter. Sector investing can indeed be risky, even in the long term. For example, a long-term investment in railroad stocks in the early part of this century seemed like a sure thing. But many blue-chip companies in that sector went bankrupt or were taken over for pennies per dollar invested. An individual sector of the market, especially if it's highly focused, can be both a short-term and a long-term drain on a portfolio. Old-line steel companies are a more recent example of an industry that can struggle and dwindle over the years. Today, oil stocks are seen as a sure thing and a great long-term investment. But imagine a world of electric automobiles and solar-powered factories. What would that do to the oil sector? Although the possibility certainly seems unlikely, we can envision a world that is far less reliant on petroleum than it is now. With that possibility, investing too heavily in oil stocks could be quite dangerous, even for the long term.

To mute the risks inherent in sector investing, it is important to think hard about what sectors of the market seem likely to remain with us. For instance, can anyone imagine a world without technology? Are we going back to the horse and buggy or the abacus? Is the computer just a fad? Of course not: technology is here to stay. And although extremely volatile in the short term, technology seems an obvious choice for long-term investing. Still, picking the overall technology winners is a daunting task, and becoming too narrowly focused in the technology sector can be extremely risky, even in the long term.

Investing in biotechnology stocks was all the rage in the late 1980s and early 1990s. These stocks were the proverbial darlings of Wall Street. But since 1991, biotechnology stocks have floundered, while technology as a whole has done well. For example, the Fidelity Select Biotechnology fund, up 99% in 1991, averaged 3.7% from 1992 to 1997. The broader market, as measured by the S&P 500, returned 19% yearly during those same six years, and the broadly diversified T. Rowe Price Science and Technology fund returned 25.1% annually.

At a 3.7% average for six years, $10,000 grows to $12,219; at 19%, $10,000 becomes $26,416; and at 25.1%, $10,000 grows to $34,919. So if at the end of 1991 you had only a six-year time horizon, biotechs would not have been the place to invest. Choosing the broadly diversified Price Science and Technology fund over the much more narrowly focused Fidelity Select Biotechnology fund would have netted an extra $22,700. That difference would buy a whole lot of extra groceries in retirement.

So rather than becoming too narrowly focused in a particular subsector, the safer, wiser approach is stay sufficiently broad within those sectors of the market that will almost certainly continue to be part of a free market economy for years to come. Thus, instead of investing strictly in oil-related stocks, choose the energy sector as a whole. For while it is possible to foresee a world with reduced oil use, it is nearly impossible to forecast a world that doesn't continually increase its demand for energy. As you read the following chapters, keep in mind that broad diversification within each sector is a wise risk reduction strategy.

The three sectors most favored by investors are financial services, health care, and technology. As a result, their stock prices are fairly expensive. Therefore, it may pay to carefully consider the other four, more out-of-favor sectors featured in this book: energy (and other natural resources), internationals, real estate, and utilities. And while short-term volatility is an inherent component of sector investing, the seven sectors highlighted here offer unique opportunities to fulfill an important component of an aggressive investor's overall portfolio.

Terms Associated with Risk (Fluctuation)

In the professional investment world, there are many terms associated with risk. What these terms actually measure is fluctuation. As we have stated earlier, fluctuation is not the same as risk. Still, given the choice, most of us would rather see our retirement nest egg always increase at a steady pace, rather than fluctuate wildly, even if the net results were the same. So let's take a moment to educate ourselves briefly on the three main terms used to measure fluctuation.

RESEARCH TIP

For a comprehensive list of investment terminology and definitions, visit the World Wide Web at www.investorwords.com. This site features a glossary of 4,000 investing terms and 15,000 links to related words.

Beta

Beta is a measurement of a stock or mutual fund's fluctuation relative to the market as a whole. A benchmark is used as a standard of comparison for an individual stock or mutual fund. For the United States, the S&P 500 index is the one most often cited. The benchmark's beta is assigned a number. The assigned number is typically 1.0. Thus, if a stock or fund has a beta of 1.3, then it has historically fluctuated 30% more than the benchmark. A beta of .80 indicates that the stock or fund is generally 20% less volatile than the overall market. It is important to note which benchmark is being used in relation to a stock or mutual fund's beta. For instance, a U.S. small-cap growth mutual fund would generally be expected to be more volatile than the S&P 500 and to have a beta significantly greater than 1.0. A more appropriate benchmark here is the Russell 2000, the best-known index of U.S. small-company stocks. That same small-cap growth fund would likely have a beta much closer to 1.0 in comparison with the fluctuations of the Russell 2000, rather than the movement of the S&P 500.

Standard Deviation

If beta measures the fluctuation of a stock, or mutual fund, against the market as a whole, then standard deviation can be said to measure the gyrations of a stock's price against itself. In other words, if a stock, or mutual fund, trades within a very narrow price range, it would have a low standard deviation. If a stock swings wildly in price from day to day, then its standard deviation would be much higher. Currently, the standard deviation for the S&P 500 index is around 18. Therefore, you would expect most individual stocks to have a higher standard deviation than 18, since individual stocks are logically more volatile than a basket of 500 stocks. By the same token, many value-oriented mutual funds have a standard deviation of less than 18, indicating that they trade in a more narrow range than the S&P 500.

Imagine that you and your spouse decide to drive to Disneyland in California for a well-deserved vacation. Much to your surprise, you find out that your next-door neighbor is planning the same trip on the same days as you. What are the odds, right? Anyway, you wave at each other as you pull out of the driveways of your suburban homes in Des Moines, Iowa, at precisely 6 a.m. on a beautiful Saturday morning. Your neighbor told you he would be stopping at a hotel two nights, but you decide to save a little money and time by driving straight through Saturday night and resting only Sunday night. You arrive at noon Monday only to bump into your neighbor at the park just as you are going through the gate.

As you chat about the trip, you find out that your neighbor did indeed stop at a hotel two different nights. Remembering your neighbor drives a Porsche, you find out he had it cranked up to around 130 miles an hour in Nevada. Your Corolla, on the other hand, never exceeded 70 miles per hour and you rarely even stopped at rest stops. So even though both of you covered the exact same miles in the exact same time with an average speed of, let's say, 50 miles an hour, your neighbor's speed fluctuated much more wildly than yours did. And that, my friend, is standard deviation. Both of you had the same average speed, but when measured against each of your own individual fluctuations in speed, we find your neighbor had a much higher standard deviation than you did. (Oh, by the way, he got a $210 speeding ticket in Colorado—if that makes you feel better.)

Standard deviation is important because it can help you determine the kind of portfolio you want. For instance, you might decide to put all your money in technology stocks, which have a higher-than-average standard deviation. That would be akin to hopping in the Porsche, stepping on the gas, and racing across the desert, realizing all the while that there may be some years when you get a ticket and returns are dismal. Or you may opt for a steadier ride, and dump all your cash in a large-company value-oriented mutual fund. Standard deviation (and beta as well) can help you make that decision.

Alpha

When measuring return against risk, two statistics are often used: alpha and the Sharpe Ratio. As noted above, beta measures a stock or fund's volatility versus the market as a whole. Alpha also measures performance against the market as a whole. However, alpha is adjusted for the level of risk as measured by beta; therefore alpha indicates how much of a stock or fund's return was due to normal market movement versus how much was based on the stock or mutual fund's unique attributes. In other words, if you had chosen to purchase five different stocks 12 months ago and were sitting on an average return of 20%, you might feel pretty good about yourself. But assuming your portfolio of these five stocks had an identical beta to the market's beta of 1.0, and the market as a whole was up 25%, then your "brilliant" stock picking actually returned 5% less than an overall average return with the same risk profile. Your portfolio therefore has an alpha of .80. And an alpha of .80 is 20% less than the 1.0 represented by the market. Your 20% return was only 80% of the market's 25% return.

Sharpe Ratio

The Sharpe Ratio is another measure of risk-adjusted returns. Developed by Nobel laureate William Sharpe, the ratio uses standard deviation as its volatility measure. The goal of the Sharpe Ratio is to determine how much excess return a mutual fund manager is adding for each unit of risk (as measured by standard deviation). Although somewhat complex, the Sharpe Ratio basically tells us about a mutual fund's historical risk-adjusted performance: the higher the Sharpe Ratio, the better the fund's risk-adjusted performance.

RESEARCH TIP

For more education on such concepts as beta, standard deviation, and the Sharpe Ratio, visit Dr. Sharpe's Web site at www.sharpe.stanford.edu.

Table 1-4 displays the standard deviation and the Sharpe Ratio for each of the open-end mutual fund managers interviewed for this book who have a three-year record at their current fund. Vanguard's S&P 500 Index fund is included as a reference point. Notice that standard deviations are quite varied. As would be expected, the technology fund swings much more wildly than the other funds, whereas utilities are the least volatile. Still, choosing a fund simply based on low volatility alone is not a good idea. The Sharpe Ratio, on the other hand, presents a much clearer picture of a fund's performance on a *risk-adjusted basis.*

According to Dr. Sharpe, Davis Real Estate, Artisan International, as well as Strong American Utilities actually outperformed Firsthand Technology Value on a risk-adjusted basis. Even though Technology Value maintained a higher three-year average return, it required considerable more volatility to achieve those extra percentage points. In the final analysis, the higher the Sharpe Ratio, the better a manager's ability to enhance returns while reducing risk.

TABLE 1-4   Three-Year Results: June 1, 1996 to May 31, 1999

Fund	3-Year Return	Standard Deviation	Sharpe Ratio
Vanguard S&P 500 Index	26.90%	21.00	1.17
Firsthand Technology Value	26.30%	49.83	.48
Strong American Utilities	20.28%	15.71	1.09
Artisan International	19.96%	23.18	.73
Davis Real Estate	13.42%	16.72	.57

Data source: Morningstar, Inc.

Are You a Sector Investor?

Is all this discussion of risk, returns, and ratios making you second-guess why you even dared to consider any type of investing, let alone sector investing? Don't be discouraged. It isn't that hard. You don't have to understand how to compute betas or Sharpe Ratios to be a sector investor. Let's face it: we are not all Nobel laureates. Few investors even look at these statistics. But if you are interested, they may give you a slight edge, especially when picking mutual funds.

If you are to become a sector investor, perhaps the three key questions to ask yourself are:

1. "Do I want to beef up my overall returns?"
2. "Am I willing to incur more volatility in order to have the potential for bigger rewards?"
3. "Do I enjoy reading and researching before I invest?"

If your answers are yes to all three questions, then you are an ideal candidate to become a sector investor. You are ready to read on. Even if you are unsure, at least read the next two chapters. They are likely to seem much simpler and more practical than the previous pages. And many of the upcoming pathways can be applied to general investing as well as sector investing.

CHAPTER 2

Pathways for Do-It-Yourself Sector Investing: Using Mutual Funds

O h good. You've turned the page. Our discussion of betas, alphas, and standard deviations has not deterred you. Our musings on the venerable nature of risk failed to sway you. *You* are a fearless investor. That, or you've got good ole capitalistic greed flowing through your veins. Whatever your motivation for continuing, it is now time to explore the pathways to sector investing.

Mutual Funds Defined

Perhaps the easiest way to become a sector investor is to buy mutual funds. In simple terms, a mutual fund is a pot of money collected from many common, ordinary investors, as well as wealthy ones. This pot of money is then placed under the control of a mutual fund manager who takes money from that pot to buy a variety of stocks and/or bonds. The result is instant diversification, because the mutual fund buyer ends up "owning" tiny pieces of lots of stocks or bonds. (Sector mutual funds are often called "specialty" or "specialized" funds.)

Just as there are star athletes, there are star mutual fund managers. They are featured in financial publications such as *Barron's, Fortune, Kiplinger's, Money,* and the *Wall Street Journal.* The key to picking sector funds, or any stock mutual fund for that matter, is to identify star managers. The theory is that just as star athletes, like Michael Jordan, put up consistently good numbers, so also will star fund managers perform consistently well.

Mutual Fund Advantages

One of the main advantages to buying mutual funds is the ability to get started with a rather small amount of money. For example, T. Rowe Price, a large no-commission investment company in Baltimore, offers its sector funds (and all others) for as little as $50 monthly, if that $50 is automatically deducted from an investor's checking account.

In addition to minimal initial money required to get started, mutual funds offer two other terrific advantages: professional investment management and diversification. By picking a sector fund, an investor hires a professional fund manager and staff focusing full time on purchasing stocks of companies offering their products and services in that particular sector. This level of in-depth knowledge and expertise in a particular sector is simply unattainable by the average investor.

The third major advantage to mutual funds is diversification. The average open-end diversified mutual fund buys about 130 stocks. Sector funds typically buy between 50 and 100 stocks. And while targeting a specific sector is higher risk than broadly diversifying one's investments across the entire market, owning a sector fund with 50 stocks is certainly lower risk than buying just one or two stocks. Lowering risk through diversification, professional management, and low minimum investment requirements makes mutual funds a preferred choice for the beginning investor.

A final advantage to mutual funds is the assurance that if you pick the right sector, you will almost always participate in the subsequent rise in its stock prices. Research on the movement of stock prices indicates that far more than 50% (some studies claim as high as 80%) of price fluctuation is specific to the industry or sector. By buying sector mutual funds, an investor only has to pick the right sector and then choose a well-managed mutual fund in that sector. The fund's diversification will ensure increased returns as the sector moves higher. But with individual stocks, that may not be the case. It is always possible to pick one or more "cold" stocks in an otherwise "hot" sector. Thus, the investor, having picked the right sector, is left out of the ensuing rise thanks to the failure of his or her stocks to move up alongside their industry brethren.

Mutual Fund Disadvantages

One of the main advantages of mutual funds can also be a disadvantage. Because mutual funds are diversified and do lower investor risk, they will never provide the terrific returns of the top individual stocks in each sector. For example, Dell Computer averaged 102.7% annually for eight and one-half years (January 1, 1990, to June 30, 1998), turning $1,000 into $405,000. During the same period, the third-best open-end mutual fund, Fidelity Select Computers, averaged 26.7%, growing $1,000 to $7,490. The only two mutual funds that had better records during that period were also Fidelity sector funds: Select Home Finance averaged 30.1% and Select Electronics returned 27.5% annually. (See Figure 2-1.)

Two other disadvantages of mutual funds, compared with individual stocks, are the capital gains tax problem and the expenses charged to operate the fund. For tax-sensitive investors, Uncle Sam's requirement that mutual funds distribute 98% of their capital gains each year to shareholders in order to avoid direct taxes on the mutual funds themselves is the biggest disadvantage. When buying an individual stock, you the investor decide when to cash in your gains. You lose that control when

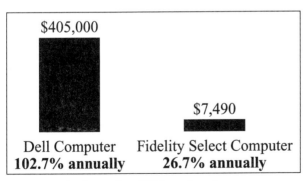

Data source: Morningstar, Inc.; *Wall Street Journal.*
FIGURE 2-1   The "Price" of Diversification:
Growth of $1,000, January 1, 1990, to June 30, 1998

buying a mutual fund; instead, the fund manager makes that sell decision, triggering capital gains that must be distributed annually to shareholders. These distributions are often done in December. Some mutual funds are more tax-efficient than others, but sector funds are noted for higher turnover that often results in significant capital gains distributions each year. One way to avoid this problem is to buy sector mutual funds in tax-advantaged accounts such as IRAs and pension funds, and then buy individual stocks in taxable accounts.

RESEARCH TIP

Morningstar has excellent tax-efficiency ratings for mutual funds. Go to your public library or visit Morningstar's Web site at www.morningstar.net. You can also subscribe to Morningstar's various publications and software packages by calling 800 735-0700.

The other major disadvantage for all mutual funds is their annual expense ratio, usually between 1% and 1.5% per year for stock mutual funds. This expense ratio covers fund operating expenses, including a manager's salary. It also provides profits for either the stockholders or the private owners of mutual fund families.

Fund Expenses

Later, we shall reveal secrets of the "loaded" fund world, including how loaded mutual fund companies can let investors put 100% of their money into a mutual fund and still pay brokers and other financial professionals their up-front commissions. But first, an exploration of how all mutual funds pay their costs and earn profits that are much higher than most other businesses is in order. All mutual funds charge expense ratios to cover their costs and provide profits to their owners. Each day the market is open, a fund's expense ratio is deducted before its net asset value (NAV) share price is calculated. The value of each fund's holdings is calculated after the market closes each day. The daily expense ratio is subtracted, and then the total remaining value is divided by the number of shares outstanding to arrive at the NAV price per share that appears in newspapers the next day. For example, a fund that charges a 1.25% expense ratio when the market is open 250 days a year would subtract 5 cents each day for each $1,000 in the fund. (See Table 2-1.)

The average U.S. stock mutual fund charges about 1.35% annually ($1.35 per $100 invested per year). Vanguard, the second-largest U.S.

**TABLE 2-I   Mutual Fund
Daily Expense of $1,000**

$1,000	(invested)
× 1.25%	(expense ratio)
= $12.50	(annual total expense)
÷ 250	(days market is open)
= .05	(fund daily expense)

fund family (Fidelity is the largest), has expense ratios that average about .45%, which is only a third of the U.S. average. Vanguard is afforded the luxury of these exceptionally low expenses because it is uniquely organized as a cooperative, totally owned by its mutual fund investors. Fidelity, on the other hand, offers by far the widest selection of sector funds, but its higher expense ratios and 3% up-front load on its Select sector funds make them much more expensive than Vanguard's five sector funds.

A further expense began in 1981, when mutual fund companies received permission from the U.S. Securities and Exchange Commission (SEC), under Ruling 12(b-1), to add fees to their funds' annual expense ratios for advertising, sales, and marketing costs. Some no-load companies and all loaded (commission-sold) mutual fund companies include 12(b-1) charges as part of their overall expense ratios. For no-load fund families, the SEC caps 12(b-1) fees that may be used for advertising and distribution at one-quarter of 1 percent (.25%) annually. Many no-load companies use their 12(b-1) fees to help pay discount brokers (Schwab, Waterhouse, E-Trade, etc.) to sell their funds without transaction fees. The SEC permits loaded mutual fund companies to levy 12(b-1) fees four times higher, up to 1% annually. This extra 1% is used both for advertising and for paying commissions to the loaded fund's sales force.

Load Versus No-Load Funds

Unfortunately, many of us have a load to bear, some burden that weighs us down. And as in life, mutual fund loads can be burdensome. They often weigh down investment returns. In the investment world, a load is simply a commission or sales charge that is added on to the cost of buying a mutual fund.

So then, what is a no-load fund and why is it superior? A no-load mutual fund is one that does *not* (1) charge a "load" fee or sales fee, (2) extract marketing and distribution fees from the fund annually that exceed .25%, (3) pay commissions, or (4) include a redemption fee (payable to the fund company) for more than a year. "No-loads" are usually not sold by stockbrokers or banks because there is no way to pay commissions to their salespeople. No-load (no-commission) mutual fund companies sell their open-end funds either directly through their toll-free numbers or through discount brokers (Schwab, Waterhouse, etc.). Commission intermediaries (full-service brokers, banks, most financial planners, etc.) sell their funds "loaded" with either up-front fees or redemption penalties up to six years. Everything else being equal, no-loads are superior because there is no additional expense to buy them and 100% of invested cash goes immediately to work, rather than having a portion of it go into a salesperson's pocket.

Open-End Funds

There were fewer than 150 open-end sector mutual funds at the end of 1993; today there are more than 300 as fund companies (often called mutual fund families) compete to offer increasingly popular "specialty" funds. Open-end mutual funds are what most investors understand as synonymous with the whole mutual fund business. Heavy advertising by industry titans—Fidelity, T. Rowe Price, Merrill Lynch, to name three of the biggest—touts the merits of these funds, adding to the popularity of open-end funds.

All open-end mutual funds create or destroy shares daily, whether "no-load" or "loaded." If XYZ fund sells $1 million of its shares to investors in one day, has $400,000 in redemptions that very same day, and closes that day at a share price of $10, then 60,000 new shares of XYZ are created. ($1,000,000 − $400,000 = $600,000, and $600,000 ÷ $10 per share = 60,000 new shares). If the numbers above are reversed, with XYZ suffering $1,000,000 in redemptions versus $400,000 in sales, then 60,000 shares are destroyed at the share closing price of $10. Simply put, open-end mutual funds are always creating shares (positive cash inflows) or destroying shares (net redemptions) each business day.

In an odd twist to open-end mutual funds, Fidelity Select's sector funds create or destroy shares hourly throughout the day. When the market is open, these funds can be bought or sold at 10:00, 11:00, 12:00, 1:00, 2:00, 3:00, and like all other mutual funds, when the market closes at 4 p.m. The catch is that Fidelity charges a 3% up-front load to buy any of its 40 Fidelity Select sector choices and a $7.50 fee to sell one if it is held for more than 30 days. Any Select fund redeemed in 30 days or less incurs a .75% charge on the entire amount sold, subject to a $7.50 minimum. If a Fidelity fund holder has already paid a 3% load on any other Fidelity fund (e.g., Magellan) and money from that fund is transferred to buy a Select fund, then the 3% load fee is waived and only a $7.50 fee is charged. However, there is yet another choice—buying closed-end mutual funds that are rarely advertised and trade on the stock exchanges.

Closed-End Funds

Instead of buying newly created open-end shares, investors can purchase closed-end fund shares on the stock exchanges just like any other stock. But these shares can be bought only from other investors who are willing to sell. Thus, closed-end mutual funds are entirely different from their open-end cousins in that the number of shares does not vary. With the launch of a new closed-end fund, investment companies sell a set number of shares on the stock exchanges through initial public offerings (IPOs), and then those shares trade just like any other stock. In other words, closed-end fund ABC, after its IPO, can be bought only through a broker from another investor willing to sell his or her shares.

The number of new closed-end stock fund IPOs offered since 1995 has declined to fewer than four per year (39 were created in 1993 and 1994) as increasingly savvy investors have learned to avoid them. Why? Typically, closed-end fund IPOs have included a 7% to 8% setup charge, barely under the maximum $8^{1}/2$% permitted by U.S. law. These exorbitant charges provide start-up money for the funds and pay generous commissions to brokers to market them. After gullible investors buy the IPOs, often priced at $15 per share, the funds begin to trade on the stock exchanges. Once the 7% to 8% in fees is subtracted, funds that were sold for $15 a share have a net asset value (NAV) of a little less than $14 a share.

> Net asset value (NAV) for closed-end funds is calculated just as it is
> for open-end funds. At the end of each trading day and after the
> expense ratio is subtracted, the total worth of the fund's holdings is
> simply divided by the number of fund shares. But unlike open-end
> funds, closed-end funds usually publish weekly, not daily, NAVs.

The problem is that most investors, and even some brokers, don't
understand that closed-end funds rarely sell at NAV when they trade on
the stock exchanges. Usually they sell at a discount. For example, if ABC
fund rises to $20 a share NAV two years after its IPO, but it trades on the
New York Stock Exchange (NYSE) at $17 per share, then it is selling at a
15% discount. ($20 − $17 = $3 and $3 ÷ $20 = 15%.) If the NAV
remained at $20 but the fund's shares sold at $23, then it would sell at a
15% premium. The reasons a closed-end fund may sell at a discount
include (1) poor past performance, (2) general bearishness regarding the
market as a whole or a particular segment of the market, (3) loss of interest by investment professionals following the IPO, (4) high expenses, and
(5) negative investor sentiment because the fund holds derivatives or illiquid securities. The reasons a closed-end fund may sell at a premium
include (1) general exuberance over a particular sector of the market, (2)
outstanding reputation of the fund manager, and (3) limited opportunity to
participate in a specific market, such as an individual country fund.

RESEARCH TIP

To find out if a particular fund is selling at a premium or a discount,
check the list of all closed-end funds that appears every Monday in the
Wall Street Journal and *Barron's*. There you will find each fund's premium or discount as well as its total return for the past 12 months.

The three basic rules that should be followed when buying or selling
closed-end funds are:

1. Don't buy a closed-end fund at the IPO (initial public offering).

2. Don't buy a closed-end fund unless its sells for at least a 10% discount.

3. Sell when a closed-end fund reaches a premium of 5% or more.

An example of how these rules can enhance returns began in February
1996, when we bought the closed-end John Hancock Bank and Thrift

Opportunity fund (symbol BTO) at a significant discount of 18%. After its sensational performance in 1997, when its NAV rose 61%, we sold it at a 14% premium in January 1998. As a result, we netted a 32% gain on the shift from the 18% discount to a 14% premium *plus all the appreciation in its NAV.* Later, in 1998, we bought it back at a 16% discount as bank stocks tanked during the August freefall in the U.S. stock market. At the end of 1998, the discount had already narrowed to 7%.

Additional Closed-End Advantages

In addition to being available to purchasers at a discount, closed-end funds offer two other advantages over their open-end cousins. Closed-end fund managers are able to remain more fully invested than open-end managers, since they never have to worry about redemptions. And because they have a stable pool of assets, closed-end managers can be truly long-term investors. Thus, they are able to buy thinly traded, more volatile securities, such as those traded only in emerging markets. Investors who want to specialize in single-country emerging-markets mutual funds often have no other choice than to buy closed-ends. For example, the only two funds specializing in buying stocks in Chile and Turkey are closed-end funds. Both funds trade on the New York Stock Exchange. One final caveat: sometimes it is possible to buy a star manager's closed-end fund when his or her open-end fund is either closed to new investors or is more expensive to buy because of commission charges.

WEBS

Another way to buy single-country closed-end mutual funds is by purchasing World Equity Benchmark Shares (WEBS) on the American Stock Exchange. Created in 1996, WEBS now represent 17 countries, including three—the Netherlands, Belgium, and Sweden—that do not have traditional closed-end equivalents.

WEBS are single-country baskets of stocks, weighted by market value. They function much like the S&P 500 index in the United States, except they have far fewer than 500 stocks. Although they trade just like closed-end funds and other stocks, they resemble open-end funds in that new shares are created (or destroyed) daily. As a result, they always trade close to their net asset value (NAV).

Warning
As a rule, closed-end funds need far more attention than open-end funds and are more appropriate for active traders. Open-ends are easier to monitor and probably best for investors who prefer to "buy and hold." Beginning sector investors may want to focus exclusively on open-ends for a "core" portfolio before branching into closed-ends as they gain more experience.

Because WEBS are index mutual funds that require only a computer program to buy or sell the stocks they hold, expense ratios are usually much lower than for traditional single-country closed-end mutual funds. Expense ratios for WEBS average 1.25%, whereas traditional closed-end country funds average about 1.80%. Also, WEBS are much more tax-efficient. There is no danger of being saddled with someone else's capital gains.

WEBS are almost always a better choice than other single-country closed-end funds if the comparable closed-end fund is selling at a premium. For example, wanting to bet on a Malaysian recovery in 1998, we twice profited by buying Malaysian WEBS selling at NAV rather than the Malaysia Fund selling at more than a 40% premium.

The final advantage of WEBS, and all closed-ends for that matter, comes from an unusual source: volatility. Closed-ends are almost always far more subject to shifts in market sentiment and, as a result, far more volatile than open-ends. Normally seen as a liability, this volatility provides opportunities for the wise investor to make more money by buying on the exaggerated dips. But it also means that closed-end funds are usually riskier than open-ends.

SPDRs

In the world of attics, spiders share an obvious relationship to webs. The same is true in the investment world. SPDRs (pronounced spiders) stands for Standard and Poor's Depository Receipts and work much the same way as WEBS. With the SPDRs, however, the basket of stocks being traded is the S&P 500 index. In 1999, Merrill Lynch began offering sector SPDRs, dividing the S&P 500 up into nine sectors to allow investors to buy their favorite sector throughout the day. Traded on the AMEX, the nine "Select Sector SPDR funds" with their trading symbols are:

Basic Industries Select Sector SPDR (XLB)

Consumer Services Select Sector SPDR (XLV)

Consumer Staples Select Sector SPDR (XLP)

Cyclical/Transportation Select Sector SPDR (XLY)

Energy Select Sector SPDR (XLE)

Financial Select Sector SPDR (XLF)

Industrial Select Sector SPDR (XLI)

Technology Select Sector SPDR (XLK)

Utilities Select Sector SPDR (XLU)

Using Discount Brokers

Everybody likes a discount. There's something about the feeling that we're getting a bargain that just lifts our mood. Using discount brokers can give us much the same feeling without sacrificing much, if any, service. Closed-end funds, just like other stocks, are now much cheaper to buy through discount brokers using Internet trading.

Investors purchase open-end mutual funds without commissions primarily by "doing it themselves." They either contact the sponsoring fund family by registering at its Web site or calling its 800 number or they may buy no-loads from discount brokers. Schwab, Jack White, Waterhouse, E-Trade, and Fidelity Brokerage have the largest number of funds (1,000 or more) in their no-load, "no transaction fee" fund supermarkets. Prior to 1992, when Schwab invented the supermarket approach, no-loads could be bought only directly from their sponsors.

Certainly the biggest innovation of this decade in the mutual fund world was Schwab's "supermarket approach," which is now widely copied by most other discount brokerages and some banks and mutual fund companies. This innovation makes it possible to buy a variety of mutual funds from different fund families in one consolidated IRA or taxable account. It also enables investors to buy and sell mutual funds from different no-load fund families 24 hours a day, seven days a week. If a no-load fund family is willing to pay Schwab or another discount broker's annual fees (Schwab typically charges a fund company .35% of its assets invested through Schwab) to market and sell its funds, then no transaction fees (NTF) are charged. In other words, an NTF fund can be bought and sold as cheaply from Schwab or other discount brokers as it can from the sponsoring mutual fund family. If the no-load fund family chooses not to pay a discount broker to sell its funds, then brokerage transaction fees are charged whenever the fund is bought or sold. Schwab's minimum of $39 is the highest; other discount brokers charge less, usually between $25 and $30.

A major disadvantage of the discount brokerages' no-load supermarket programs are that they must limit excessive trading to make a profit. Therefore, Schwab charges a transaction on any NTF funds not held for at least six months. Jack White and E-Trade require only a 90-day wait. Waterhouse and Fidelity have a six-month holding period, but will allow up to four free NTF sells annually of funds not held at least six months. Especially disheartening is that Fidelity, T. Rowe Price, and Vanguard, the three biggest no-load fund families with the most sector funds available, do not offer their funds without transaction fees through other discount brokerages. However, for the serious "do-it-yourself" mutual fund investor, the supermarket no-load mutual fund approach is by far the easiest way to invest.

Share Classes

Full-service brokers, almost all bank and insurance sales representatives, and many financial planners sell "loaded" funds; they get paid commissions from the mutual fund companies and/or insurance companies they represent. Mutual funds sponsored and sold by insurance companies are called variable annuities. Prior to the 1990s, most commission-generating mutual funds were sold with a "front-end load." Many of them carried sales charges of 8.75%—the maximum sales charge permitted by U.S. law. An 8.75% sales charge means that for each $100 invested, only $91.25 actually purchases mutual fund shares.

Today, 8.75% is rarely charged. As competition intensified, the upfront load declined to the new standard, less than 6%. The largest loaded fund company, Merrill Lynch, currently charges 5.25%; the next two largest, Putnam and American funds, charge 5.75% for almost all their stock funds. Shares with up-front loads are typically listed as class A shares, and once purchased may be sold at any time without charge.

In time, many investors began to rebel against paying even reduced up-front fees; as a result, the loaded fund families were forced to create a different share class. Usually labeled as class B shares, this share class allows 100% of the investor's money to go toward purchasing mutual fund shares. Thus, no commission is taken off the top. However, since all the money is immediately invested, the problem for the loaded fund families becomes one of recouping the up-front commissions they must continue to pay in order to motivate salespeople to push their funds.

Enter a rather ingenious solution: charge much higher 12(b-1) expense fees for class B shares than class A shares. Thus, the loaded mutual funds are able to slowly recapture the initial money they pay to their representatives when the fund is sold by subtracting higher expense ratios each day for class B shares. Enter another problem for the commission-sold fund companies: this slow recapture method makes economic sense only if investors keep their money in the fund family long enough for the fund company to recoup the commission money initially paid.

Enter another solution: the creation of redemption penalties, also called "back-end loads" or deferred sales charges. In most cases, investors must keep their money with the fund company for up to five years before they are permitted to sell out without penalty and invest the proceeds elsewhere. A typical back-end load redemption schedule of a newly purchased fund is displayed in Table 2-2.

For some funds, penalty fees linger even longer than five years. It takes six years before class B Dean Witter funds' penalty fees disappear, and most insurance company mutual funds, called variable annuities, have redemption penalty fees that continue for seven years. Please note

TABLE 2-2   Typical Schedule for Back-End Loads

Years Since Initial Purchase of Fund	Percentage Redemption Charge
Less than 1 year	5%
1–2 years	4%
2–3 years	3%
3–4 years	2%
4–5 years	1%
5 years or more	0%

that redemption fees apply only if money is redeemed from a fund before the designated penalty period has elapsed and that money is *not* immediately reinvested into another fund sponsored by the same fund company. In other words, an investor may sell one Putnam class B share and buy another Putnam fund or sell a Merrill Lynch class B fund and buy another Merrill Lynch fund without triggering back-end loads. But that same investor is not allowed to sell a Putnam class B fund penalty-free to buy a Merrill Lynch class B fund during the penalty period even if both funds are handled by the same Merrill Lynch broker.

Even though a fund has two classes of shares, A and B, the makeup of the fund is almost exactly the same. In other words, the manager normally buys the same stocks for all classes of a fund. The only difference is that, after the market closes, a higher expense ratio is subtracted each day from class B shares than from class A shares. Naturally, that means the yearly returns from class B shares are always less than those from class A shares. For example, Alliance Technology fund class A has a 1.67% expense ratio and returned an average of 31.32% a year for the three years ended January 31, 1999. But its class B twin has a 2.38% expense ratio and averaged 30.41% for the same three years. The primary difference is the additional .71% (71 cents per $100 per year) that the class B share subtracts to repay Alliance for the commissions it paid to the salesperson when the fund was first sold. (See Table 2-3.)

Because investors voice so much opposition to paying initial sales fees, class B shares have become the most popular share class sold by brokers and other financial professionals. For more than six decades the highly successful American fund family (Washington Mutual, Growth Fund of America, and EuroPacific are three of its most famous funds) offered only class A shares with a front-end load (currently 5.75%). However, in 1997, after several years of turning down requests from brokers for a class B alternative, it was forced to create its own class B shares to remain competitive.

TABLE 2-3　Alliance Technology: Three Years Ending January 31, 1999

	Expense Ratio	3-Year Annual Return
Class A shares	1.67%	31.32%
Class B shares	2.38%	30.41%

Not surprisingly, class C shares were soon invented because some investors objected to both up-front fees and redemption penalty periods of five years or longer. The new class C share is typically offered with no up-front loads, very high expense ratios, and a 1% redemption fee that may never disappear. These class C shares do, on occasion, have a 1% front-end fee, and sometimes have expense ratios that are higher than class B shares. Class C shares are also seldom convertible to class A shares, no matter how long they have been held.

Finally, many loaded fund companies also have class Y or Z shares, which typically are exactly like no-loads. They have no front-end or back-end loads and have expense ratios as low as (or lower than) class A shares. Investors normally can get these shares only through money managers, who, of course, charge ongoing management fees. Alternatively, they may have bought a no-load fund prior to its becoming a loaded fund, usually as a result of a buyout by a loaded fund company. This then would grandfather investors into the more attractive class Y or Z shares. Class Y or Z funds often have minimum investment requirements of $100,000 or more for new retail investors, or they are exclusively sold in large chunks to institutional investors.

Which Class?

No-loads are by far the best choice for most investors. But for investors contemplating the purchase of loaded mutual funds through a broker or bank, which class share is the best choice? Obviously, class Y or Z is the best choice, but these funds are rarely available to the average investor. If class C funds are available and a move to a different fund family within three years seems likely, then they may be the best choice.

Typically, the choice boils down to class A or class B shares. Class B shares will generally be a better buy when:

1. The up-front load is 5% or more.
2. The redemption penalty period is five years or less.
3. The expense ratio is no more than .8% higher for class B shares.
4. The market is returning 13% or less. (The market's historical norm since World War II has been a 12.5% annual return.)

Still, investors who hate being "trapped" in a fund family for five years or more certainly should consider purchasing the class A shares.

Deceptive Practices

All this talk of share classes can be very confusing. Unfortunately, a few deceptive practices by some representatives of the financial services industry have added to the confusion. For example, when loaded funds are sold, some financial professionals do not fully explain that class B shares carry those five-year (or longer) redemption penalties. They expect their clients to read it in the fine print. A few go so far as to violate federal law by telling clients that they can sell class B shares "no load." If a fund family has different share classes, then it is *not* selling its funds "no-load." A possible exception is if that fund company has an institutional fund that requires a very large purchase.

Another example, even more common, is for a loaded fund sales rep to tell prospective clients that no-load funds have higher expense ratios. In fact, exactly the opposite is true. According to Morningstar, the typical no-load stock fund charges about .3% (30 cents per $100 per year) less for its expense ratio than its loaded counterpart. Unscrupulous financial professionals may go so far as to assert that "no-loads have higher management fees." But management fees are part of the expense ratio. The expense ratio is the key, because that is the only way that mutual fund companies get paid.

The Importance of Low Expenses

In the raging bull market of the 1990s, both no-load and loaded mutual fund companies have found it easy to raise expense ratios. Vanguard is the exception. The fastest-growing of the largest fund companies, Vanguard has increased its market share of U.S. mutual fund assets by 50%, from 6.5% in 1990 to 9.8% in 1999. And it has consistently lowered its expense ratios. No other fund company even comes close to providing the low costs that Vanguard offers. It also originated index funds, which have very low expense ratios. Its S&P 500 fund, with an expense ratio of .18%, now has more than $80 billion in assets, trailing only Fidelity Magellan in size. One reason for Vanguard's low-cost structure is its status as a nonprofit owned by the investors who buy its mutual fund shares.

Expenses are extremely important in selecting a mutual funds. A one-half percent difference in a mutual fund expense ratio doesn't seem very significant if the market is returning 20% a year. After all, that's only

$2^1/2\%$ of the annual return. However, if the market is returning 10% a year, that half-point extra expense eats up 5% of the annual return. The best advice is to buy no-loads whenever possible with expense ratios less than the national average of 1.35%. With sector funds, particularly promising new sector funds, expense ratios up to 2% are acceptable. A star manager opening a new fund is typically a fine choice, even though expense ratios are often higher than average. As the new fund grows larger, it should significantly lower its expense ratio.

As funds grow too large, though, several problems invariably emerge. First, even though their expense ratio drops, their trading costs, which are not included in the expense ratio, grow ever larger. Second, it becomes much more difficult for managers to take meaningful positions in smaller stocks. Finally, even with midcaps and larger companies, huge block trades, the cheapest to execute, can actually move buy prices higher or sell prices lower. Consequently, higher buy prices when a fund manager is attempting to acquire a large block of a particular stock and lower sell prices when the manager is trying to dump a block of stock obviously translate into lower profits for investors.

The Importance of Fund Managers

Paying attention to expense ratios and understanding that funds may grow too large are important considerations when picking a mutual fund. Still, the most important criterion for picking a stock mutual fund is the talent of the lead manager or management team and the capability of the analysts and traders employed. But how can that talent be judged? The simplest way is to look at the manager's track record. Does the fund manager have a documented history of leading a fund, especially during bear markets? If so, how does that record compare with market averages?

Most financial magazines routinely print a list of top mutual funds for one year, three years, and five years. But rarely do they note whether the fund manager or management team that established that record is still in place. Star mutual fund managers are becoming hot commodities. Like star athletes who move from one team to another, they can bounce around like free agents. So in recognition of the importance of a prior record, the SEC now permits fund companies to advertise a manager's performance at a previous fund. Specialized mutual fund newsletters often secure the documented statistics of a manager who was in charge of private and/or institutional accounts. They add an appropriate expense ratio and are often able to piece together a 10-year or longer statistical history, which then is compared with appropriate market benchmarks.

A word of caution here: don't dump a manager just because of one bad year. Just as star athletes are bedeviled by slumps, star managers may have a lousy year too. Often that happens when their investment style is out of favor or, as has been the case since 1994 with small-company stocks, when another asset class (currently large-company stocks) dominates. One problem is that investors often compare their mutual funds against the S&P 500 or the Dow Jones Industrial Average—both of which are large-company indexes. Small-company mutual funds should be compared against the Russell 2000, midcaps against the S&P 400, and internationals against an appropriate foreign stock index. Sector funds have their own benchmarks as well. Seven commonly accepted indices for the sectors we are tracking in this book are listed in Table 2-4.

Turnover Rates and Concentration

Two other criteria for picking mutual funds are turnover rates and concentration. Simply stated, turnover rate measures the annual percentage of a mutual fund's securities that are bought and sold. Research by Morningstar shows that high turnover (more frequent trading) of small U.S.

TABLE 2-4   Commonly Accepted Sector Indices

Sector	Index
Technology	PSE Tech 100 Index
Financial	Dow Jones Financial Index
Health care	Dow Jones Pharmaceutical Index
International	Europe, Asia, and Far East (EAFE) Index
Real estate	Wilshire REIT Index
Utilities	Dow Jones Utilities Index
Energy and resources	Dow Jones Energy Index

company funds adds value, while low turnover of large U.S. company funds is a real plus. In addition, high turnover often causes tax headaches to investors who hold their funds in a taxable account. Even if a manager adds a few percentage points to the fund's overall return by trading extensively, those returns could be muted by a sizable tax bill for the individual investor because of the annual capital gains distribution that mutual funds are required to make.

Finally, there is a growing realization that many funds are overly diversified. The average U.S. stock fund holds 130 different stocks. Critics wonder how any manager can have 130 good ideas. It seems logical that a manager's first 10 picks (numbers 1 through 10) would be better than the last 10 picks (numbers 121 to 130). As a result, more and more "focus" or "select" funds are making their debuts; they usually hold between 20 and 50 stocks. This is concentration.

Using IRAs

Even though mutual funds hold the many advantages already discussed, the problem of taxation remains a major drawback. The tax problem is negated with index funds or those funds managed for tax efficiency. Unfortunately, sector funds are often tax-inefficient because of their higher turnover rates. A high turnover rate generally signals a larger capital gains payout and thus higher taxes for the individual investor. Individual retirement accounts (IRAs) and other tax-deferred vehicles eliminate this concern and therefore are opportune places for sector investing.

There are now three types of IRAs. The tax-deductible traditional IRA, the nondeductible traditional IRA, and the new Roth IRA, named after Senator William Roth of Delaware. The contributions for the traditional tax-deductible IRA are considered pretax, and a deduction is allowed on your tax form. For tax purposes, it's like you never earned the money in the first place. With the nondeductible traditional IRA, contributions are made in after-tax dollars. No deduction is allowed at tax filing. With both the traditional deductible and nondeductible IRAs, the investment earnings grow tax-deferred, eliminating the need to worry about the tax inefficiencies of sector funds. Still, when the money is withdrawn in retirement, taxes are paid at ordinary income tax rates. This is not the case with the Roth IRA.

The Roth IRA

The Roth IRA has been much bandied about on financial talk shows and in print media alike, and for good reason. It offers unique opportunities for most all investors, especially those hoping for big gains through sector investing. The beauty of the new Roth IRA is that although the money is invested on an after-tax, nondeductible basis, there are never any taxes due when the money is used in retirement. That means there are no taxes on the buildup. This is the key advantage to the Roth IRA for the sector investor. Almost unbelievably, Uncle Sam gives all but the highest-income earners the opportunity for tax-free income. That's *tax-free,* not tax-deferred.

There are a few rules, of course. First of all, the Roth IRA account must be open for at least five years and the investor must be age $59^1/2$ or older before any of the profits from the Roth IRA can be withdrawn tax-free. But unlike the case of traditional IRAs, the *contributions* can be withdrawn without taxes or penalties at any time for any reason.

Those eligible to participate in a Roth IRA include just about everybody. As with all IRAs, the taxpayer must have earned income to participate. Dividend income does not count. A nonworking spouse can have a Roth IRA too. As long as the couple earns at least $4,000, each can have a $2,000 IRA every year. The maximum income limit for singles is $95,000 for the full $2,000 participation; singles who earn $110,000 can't have a Roth IRA at all. The full participation limit for marrieds is $150,000, with total phase-out at $160,000.

One of the disadvantages for people age $59^1/2$ and over is that the five-year waiting period to take investment gains tax-free still applies. No matter the age, the individual Roth investor still has to wait five years from January 1 of the tax year designated when the Roth account was first opened. For example, gains in a Roth IRA first opened in March 2000 for tax year 1999 could be tapped tax-free on or after January 1, 2004 for anyone age $59^1/2$ or older. One of the big advantages for younger people is that if they meet the five-year test for the Roth IRA, they can take $10,000 in capital gains out of the Roth IRA at any age to buy a first-time home. So they could use that $10,000 in profits, plus all the dollars they put into the Roth account, to buy a home. Another advantage to the Roth IRA is that, unlike the old IRAs that mandate withdrawals beginning at age $70^1/2$, the Roth IRA never requires any withdrawals. It can be kept tax-free forever. And unlike the traditional IRAs, beneficiaries inherit the Roth totally free from income taxes.

Roth Conversions

No, a Roth conversion is not some type of exalted religious experience. But a Roth conversion could, after many years, become quite uplifting for financial returns. Basically, any traditional IRA can be converted to a Roth IRA, with one major catch. Taxes due on the converted amount must be paid in the same tax year as the conversion. Deciding whether to convert to a Roth IRA and therefore pay taxes that could be deferred is a difficult decision. We suggest you contact a tax advisor or financial professional.

RESEARCH TIP

Roth analyzer software is available from T. Rowe Price for $9.95. Or for a free Roth rollover/analyzer kit, call T. Rowe Price at 800 225-5132. The best Web access for conversion analysis is www.vanguard.com. Also see www.troweprice.com.

Of course, all this talk of IRAs and tax inefficiencies become a veritable moot point for the sector investor who chooses individual stocks over sector mutual funds as the primary path to long-term wealth enhancement. But alas, selecting individual stocks is certainly a more challenging endeavor.

CHAPTER

3

Pathways for Do-It-Yourself Sector Investing: Buying Individual Stocks

I f, as we have stated in the previous chapter, mutual funds are the easiest and safest pathway for sector investing, then buying individual stocks is certainly the most exciting. Ah yes, there's just something about plunking down a couple of thousand dollars to buy a piece of GE that boils the blood. The thought of being part owner of one of the two most valuable companies in the world...well...let's just say "exhilaration" most closely captures the feeling. Granted, a $2,000 stake in GE won't even earn you the right to play an unseen extra on *Friends* (GE owns NBC), but at least you do get a share of the profits, no matter how minuscule that share might be.

Prior to the 1990s, investing in individual stocks was cost-prohibitive for the small investor. In order to buy that $2,000 worth of GE, you usually had to pay $60 or more in commissions. That meant 3% was immediately eaten up in trading costs. And even though commission schedules for the full-service main-line brokerage houses are still high, there are many new options available to the little guy. The do-it-yourselfer now is able to buy and sell stocks very inexpensively, or sometimes even for no fees at all.

DRIPs

If you have ever had a leaky faucet, you certainly understand how annoying a drip can be. The constant, almost rhythmic drops of water echoing against a stainless steel sink can, after a while, be most irritating. But when it comes to investing, dividend reinvestment plans, or DRIPs, are actually good. They enable you to invest very small amounts in many different companies without using a broker. And just like a water drip that eventually fills a bowl, DRIPs allow little chunks of money to be regularly added over time until eventually a substantial equity portfolio has been acquired. Plus, several companies offer their DRIP stocks with absolutely no fees or commissions. Here's how it works.

Dividend reinvestment plans are set up and maintained directly by the corporation in which you choose to invest. Companies offering these plans range from Exxon to Chock Full O'Nuts, Merck to Tektronix, GE to Spanish telephone company Telfonica, and many more. The specific rules differ from company to company. Some companies require that you already be a shareholder before you can join a DRIP. This means that you need to buy at least one share of stock from a broker. However, more and more companies, such as the ones mentioned above, allow you to buy even the initial share directly from the company, thereby entirely bypassing a broker.

Charles Carlson, the editor of *No-Load Stock Insider,* has dubbed this latter group "no-load stocks" because commissions are avoided altogether, although many companies do charge fees (usually a few cents a share). Minimum investments also differ from company to company. IBM, for instance, requires a $500 minimum initial investment, and at least $50 each time you add to your account. Three oil companies—Chevron, Exxon-Mobil, and Texaco—allow initial purchases for as little as $250. Some companies charge maintenance fees and check-cashing fees. Others do not. You'll want to take all these things into consideration before deciding on a particular company's DRIP. It doesn't make much sense to invest only $100 in a DRIP like McDonald's that charges a $5 check-processing fee.

Table 3-1 shows Charles Carlson's list of no-load U.S. stocks with phone numbers and minimum initial purchase requirements.

TABLE 3-1 U.S Firms That Permit Initial Purchases Directly

Company	Minimum Initial Purchase	Phone	Company	Minimum Initial Purchase	Phone
ABT Building Products	$250	800 774-4117	Associates First Capital	$1,000	888 297-6879
Aetna	$500	800 955-4741	Atmos Energy	$200	800 774-4117
AFLAC	$750	800 227-4756	Avery Dennison	$500	800 649-2291
AGL Resources	$250	800 774-4117	Bank of NY	$1,000	800 727-7033
Air Products	$500	888 694-9458	Bard (C.R.)	$250	800 828-1639
AirTouch Comm.	$500	800 727-7033	Becton, Dickinson	$250	800 955-4743
Allstate	$500	800 448-7007	Bedford Properties	$1,000	800 774-5476
American Elec. Power	$250	800 955-4740	Bell Atlantic	$1,000	800 631-2355
American Express	$1,000	800 842-7629	BellSouth	$500	888 266-6778
Ameritech	$1,000	800 774-4117	Blyth Industries	$250	877 424-1968
Amoco	$450	800 774-4117	Bob Evans Farms	$50	800 272-7675
Amway Asia Pacific	$250	800 727-7033	Borg-Warner Auto	$500	800 774-4117
Arrow Financial	$300	518 745-1000	Boston Beer	$500	888 266-6780
Ascent Entertainment	$100	800 727-7033	Bowne & Co.	$500	800 524-4458

TABLE 3-1 (*Continued*)

Company	Minimum Initial Purchase	Phone	Company	Minimum Initial Purchase	Phone
BRE Properties	$500	800 774-4117	Community Bank Sys.	$500	800 842-7629
California Water Service	$500	800 337-3503	Compaq Computer	$250	888 218-4373
Campbell Soup	$500	800 649-2160	COMSAT	$250	800 727-7033
Capstead Mortgage	$250	800 969-6715	Conectiv	$500	800 365-6495
Carpenter Technology	$500	800 822-9828	Consolidated Freightways	$100	800 727-7033
Caterpillar	$500	800 955-4749	Cross Timbers Oil	$500	800 774-4117
Central & South West	$250	800 774-4117	Crown Am. Realty Tr.	$100	800 774-4117
Central Hudson G&E (NY)	$100	888 280-3848	CSX	$500	800 774-4117
Chevron	$250	800 774-4117	Curtiss-Wright	$2,000	888 266-6793
Chock Full O'Nuts	$100	888 200-3161	Darden Restaurants	$1,000	800 829-8432
Chrysler	$1,000	800 649-9896	Dayton Hudson	$500	888 268-0203
CILCORP	$250	800 774-4117	Deere & Co.	$500	800 268-7369
CMS Energy	$500	800 774-4117	Disney (Walt)	$1,000	800 948-2222
Coastal	$250	800 788-2500	Dominion Resources	(VA)$250	800 552-4034

Company		Company	
Dow Jones & Co.	$1,000 800 842-7629	Fannie Mae	$250 888 289-3266
DQE	$105 800 247-0400	Fed One Bancorp	$250 800 742-7540
DTE Energy	$100 800 774-4117	Finova Group	$500 800 774-4117
Duke Energy	$250 800 488-3853	First Financial Holdings	$250 800 998-9151
Duke Realty	$250 800 774-4117	FirstEnergy	$250 800 736-3402
Eastern Co.	$250 800 633-3455	FIRSTPLUS Financial	$1,000 800 842-7629
Eastman Kodak	$150 800 253-6057	Food Lion	$250 888 232-9530
EMCEE Broadcast	$100 888 200-3167	Ford Motor	$1,000 800 955-4791
Energen	$250 800 774-4117	Frontier Insurance	$100 888 200-3162
Enova	$250 800 307-7343	GenCorp	$500 800 727-7033
Enron	$250 800 662 7662	General Electric	$250 800 786-2543
Entergy	$1,000 800 225-1721	General Growth Prop.	$200 800 774-4117
Equifax	$500 888 887-2971	Gillette	$1,000 800 643-6989
Equitable Cos.	$500 800 437-8736	Glenborough Realty	$250 800 266-6785
Equity Residential	$250 800 337-5666	Glimcher Realty	$100 800 738-4931
Essex Property	$100 800 945-8245	Goodyear	$250 800 453-2440
Exxon	$250 800 252-1800	Green Mt. Power	$50 802 864-5731

TABLE 3-1 *(Continued)*

Company	Minimum Initial Purchase	Phone	Company	Minimum Initial Purchase	Phone
GreenPoint Financial	$2,000	800 842-7629	Johnson Controls	$50	800 524-6220
Guidant	$250	800 537-1677	Justin Industries	$500	800 727-7033
Harland (John H.)	$500	800 649-2202	Kaman	$250	800 842-7629
Hawaiian Electric Inds.	$250	808 543-5662	Kellwood	$100	314 576-3100
Hillenbrand Inds.	$250	800 774-4117	Kerr-McGee	$750	800 395-2662
Home Depot	$250	800 774-4117	Lear	$250	800 727-7033
Home Properties	$2,000	800 774-4117	Libbey	$100	800 727-7033
Houston Industries	$250	800 774-4117	Liberty Property Trust	$1,000	800 944-2214
IBM	$500	888 421-8860	Lilly (Eli)	$1,000	800 451-2134
Illinova	$250	800 750-7011	Longs Drug Stores	$500	888 213-0886
Interchange Fin'l Svcs.	$100	201 703-2265	Lucent Technologies	$1,000	800 774-4117
Interstate Energy	$250	800 356-5343	Macerich	$250	800 567-0169
Investors Financial	$250	888 333-5336	Madison Gas & Electric	$50	800 356-6423
IPALCO Enterprises	$250	800 774-4117	Mallinckrodt	$500	800 446-2617

Company	Amount	Phone	Company	Amount	Phone
Mattel	$500	888 909-9922	NationsBank	$1,000	800 642-9855
McDonald's	$1,000	800 774-4117	Nationwide Financial Svcs.	$500	800 409-7514
MCN Energy	$250	800 955-4793	New England Business Svc.	$250	800 736-3001
MDU Resources	$50	701 222-7991	Newport	$100	888 200-3169
Meadowbrook Insurance	$250	800 649-2579	Newport News Ship	$500	800 649-1861
Mellon Bank	$500	800 842-7629	Norwest	$250	800 774-4117
Mercantile Bancorp.	$500	800 774-4117	OGE Energy	$250	800 774-4117
Merck	$350	800 774-4117	Old National Bancorp	$500	800 774-4117
Meritor Automotive	$500	800 483-2277	Oneok	$100	800 395-2662
Michaels Stores	$500	800 577-4676	Owens Corning	$1,000	800 472-2210
MidAmerican Energy	$250	800 247-5211	Penney (J.C.)	$250	800 565-2576
MidSouth Bancorp	$1,000	800 842-7629	Peoples Energy	$250	800 774-4117
Minnesota P&L	$250	800 774-4117	Pharmacia & Upjohn	$250	800 774-4117
Mobil	$250	800 648-9291	Philadelphia Subrn	$500	800 774-4117
Morgan Stanley	$1,000	800 228-0829	Phillips Petroleum	$500	888 887-2968
Morton Int'l	$1,000	800 774-4117	Piedmont Natural Gas	$250	800 774-4117
National Service Inds.	$600	888 836-5069	Pinnacle West (AZ)	$50	800 774-4117

TABLE 3-1 *(Continued)*

Company	Minimum Initial Purchase	Phone	Company	Minimum Initial Purchase	Phone
Procter & Gamble	$250	800 764-7483	Sanderson Farms	$500	800 842-7629
Providian Financial	$500	800 482-8690	SBC Communications	$500	888 836-5062
Public Service Enterprise	$250	800 242-0813	SCANA	$250	800 763-5891
Public Service of New Mexico	$50	800 545-4425	Schnitzer Steel	$500	800 727-7033
Public Service of NC	$250	800 774-4117	Sears, Roebuck & Co.	$500	888 732-7788
Quaker Oats	$500	800 774-4117	Security Capital Pacific	$200	800 842-7629
Quanex	$250	800 278-4353	SEMCO Energy	$250	800 649-1856
Questar	$250	800 729-6788	SIS Bancorp	$1,000	888 877-2891
Reader's Digest	$1,000	800 242-4653	Snap-on	$500	800 501-9474
Redwood Trust	$500	800 774-4117	Sonoco Products	$250	800 864-2246
Regions Financial	$500	800 922-3468	Southern Co.	$250	800 774-4117
Roadway Express	$250	800 774-4117	Southern Union	$250	800 793-8938
Robbins & Myers	$500	800 622-6757	Storage Trust	$250	800 842-7629
Rockwell Int'l	$1,000	800 842-7629	Sunstone Hotel Inv.	$1,000	800 774-4117

Company	Min.	Phone	Company	Min.	Phone
Synovus Financial	$250	800 337-0896	Valspar	$1,000	800 842-7629
Tandy	$250	888 218-4374	Wal-Mart Stores	$250	800 438-6278
Taubman Centers	$250	800 774-4117	Walgreen	$50	800 774-4117
Tektronix	$500	800 842-7629	Warner-Lambert	$250	888 767-7166
Tenneco	$500	800 519-3111	Weingarten Realty	$500	888 887-2966
Texaco	$250	800 283-9785	Western Resources	$250	800 774-4117
Thornburg Mortgage Asset	$500	800 509-5586	Westvaco	$250	800 432-9874
Timken	$1,000	888 347-2453	Whirlpool	$1,000	800 409-7442
TNP Enterprises	$100	800 774-4117	Whitman	$250	800 660-4187
Transocean Offshore	$500	800 727-7033	WICOR	$500	800 236-3453
Tribune	$500	800 924-1490	Wisconsin Energy	$50	800 558-9663
Tyson Foods	$250	800 822-7096	WLR Foods	$250	540 896-7001
U S West Comm Grp.	$300	800 537-0222	WPS Resources	$100	800 236-1551
United Wisconsin Svcs.	$100	414 276-3737	XXSYS Technologies	$100	888 200-3166
Urban Shopping Ctrs.	$500	800 774-4117	York International	$1,000	800 774-4117
UtiliCorp United	$250	800 647-2789			

Source: Charles Carlson, "DRIP List (for November–December 1998)" *No Load Stock Insider*, December 1998.

RESEARCH TIP

For a free sample issue of Charles Carlson's newsletter, *No-Load Stock Insider,* call 219 852-3230. For a complete list of DRIPs, contact the *Money Paper* at 800 495-1992 and ask for the *Guide to Dividend Reinvestment Plans.* It will cost you about $12.

The following is a list of steps for investing in DRIPs:

1. Request information on the DRIPs in which you are interested by calling the toll-free number provided by the company or its processing agent, or by visiting the company's Web site.

2. Decide if that company plan meets your investment objectives. (Remember, DRIPs are primarily for long-term accumulation, not for trading.)

3. Make certain the fees are reasonable. (Is there a charge to open or close an account? What are the fees per share to buy or sell? Is there a yearly maintenance fee?)

4. Find out investment minimums. (What is the minimum to open an account? What is the minimum additional amount accepted by check or automatic checking account draft?)

5. Fill out the application and send in a check with the application form.

As you can see, investing in DRIPs is a fairly straightforward and simple process. Still, there are both advantages and disadvantages to these plans.

DRIP Advantages

We have already alluded to the major DRIP advantage. DRIPs enable you to buy stock without paying commissions. This commission-free trading applies to purchases of 10 shares or 10,000 shares. For the larger investor, the commission savings can be considerable. For example, Charles Schwab, a discount broker, charges approximately $971 by phone (or $150 over the Internet) to buy 5,000 shares of a $160 dollar stock when using a live broker. That $971 (or $150) charge would be totally eliminated if you invested through a DRIP that charges no fees to buy its stock.

Another advantage is that with most DRIPs, convenient automatic monthly checking account drafts are an option. For the smaller investor, this is an easy way to dollar-cost-average over long periods of time. But one of the real advantages of DRIPs and other purchases of individual stocks is that there are no capital gains taxes until you decide to sell. With mutual funds, by contrast, at least some capital gains are paid out annually. The only taxes you pay annually on DRIP investments are on the quarterly dividends the company pays out. Thus, choosing companies with very low dividend payouts can really pay off come April 15. Also, a few DRIPs, such as Exxon-Mobil, even permit traditional IRA accounts (tax-deductible money grows tax-deferred until retirement) or Roth IRAs (after-tax investments grow tax-free forever).

DRIP Disadvantages

Disadvantages of DRIP purchases begin with the fact that companies make purchases or sales only periodically—usually weekly, semimonthly, or monthly. As a result, you never know the exact buy or sell price until well after the purchase or sale. Therefore, DRIPs are best for long-term accumulation and not short-term trading. Another disadvantage is that many companies (Abbott Labs and Delta Airlines, to name just two) offer only the old-fashioned, traditional DRIPs that require you to own at least one share of the company's stock before you can become a participant. It can certainly be a nuisance to buy just one share of stock, have it issued out to you (brokerage-held stocks are ineligible for DRIPs), and then be forced to keep the stock certificates in a safe place. Also, the whole process takes several weeks before you become eligible for a DRIP.

The biggest headache with DRIPs comes when you get ready to sell the stock. First of all, it can be a painstakingly slow process. Typically, you must fill out a redemption slip, sign your name, mail in the slip, and then wait for a check (usually 10 days to two weeks). But as annoying as the redemption process can be, there is a bigger headache. Since you most likely have bought your shares over a long period of time and at many different prices (because of dollar cost averaging) figuring out your profit or loss can be difficult. You will need to keep careful records of each purchase, including the number of shares purchased, the price per share, and the date of each purchase. Good records make figuring those capital gains or losses a much less taxing process.

Discount Brokers, Deep-Discount Brokers, and the Internet

If you want to buy and sell stocks annually or even more frequently, or if you want more control over the buy and sell price of your individual stocks, then DRIPs surely are not for you. But do not despair; you need not be relegated to the big brokerage houses—forced to pay hefty commissions. The discount brokers and online trading are here to save the day!

Discount brokers started to take off in the 1970s and have never looked back. Offering stock trading at a reduced cost was the hallmark of the discounters, such as Charles Schwab and Waterhouse Securities. But with reduced cost came reduced service. As a result, many investors who required occasional hand holding and advice stayed with the big, established brokerages. For the do-it-yourself investor, though, the reduced cost of the discount brokers was so enticing that it led to the next wave of cost cutting: deep discounting.

Offering almost no frills, deep-discount brokerages rolled out what seem to be impossibly low commission rates. But low got even lower. Fed by the Internet's emerging popularity, trading volume increased and rates continued to fall until finding an apparent floor at the $5 rate charged by Browne and Company. Utilizing the deep discounter's rock-bottom Internet trading rates, do-it-yourself sector investors can save big money. As Browne and Company's advertising proclaims, "$5 is not a commission, it's a tip!" Table 3-2 presents a list of the 12 largest online brokers and their lowest available rates as well as other features as of December 1998.

Buying Foreign Stocks

International investing is one of the sectors (loosely defined) that we are featuring in this book. For most people, buying stocks of corporations headquartered in foreign countries is best accomplished by investing in mutual funds. A professional manager is a big plus in the ever-changing and often ambiguous world of international equities. Still, free-spirited investors may want to delve independently into individual foreign issues. In fact, buying foreign stock is not as complex as some investors might suppose.

Many foreign companies are listed on American stock exchanges as American Depository Receipts (ADRs) and can be bought just like any other stock. For instance, Sony is a Japanese company listed as an ADR on the New York Stock Exchange. Its symbol is SNE and any market order for SNE will be executed in the same manner as for a U.S. company. Anyone wishing to play the chocolate "sector" might consider Nestlé a fine purchase, convinced that it is a U.S. company. Nestlé is actually a Swiss company, but it too is available as an ADR.

TABLE 3-2 Comparing the 12 Largest Online Brokers (ranked by number of online accounts)

Firm	Address	Online Price	Phone Help	Real-Time Quotes
Charles Schwab	www.schwab.com	$29.95 up to 1,000 shares	24 hours a day 7 days a week	200 free quotes plus 100 for each order
Fidelity Investments	www.fidelity.com	$25 market orders; $30 limit orders; up to 1,000 shares*	24 hours a day 7 days a week	Unlimited free quotes
DLJdirect	www.dljdirect.com	$20 up to 1,000 shares	7 a.m. to 1 a.m. EST weekdays; 8 a.m. to 10 p.m. weekends	100 free quotes plus 100 for each order and 500 for $19.95
E*Trade	www.etrade.com	$14.95 market orders; $19.95 limit orders; up to 5,000 shares	8 a.m. to midnight EST weekdays	Unlimited free quotes
Waterhouse Investor Services	www.waterhouse.com	$12 up to 5,000 shares	24 hours a day 7 days a week	100 free quotes plus 100 for each order and 100 for $5
Ameritrade	www.ameritrade.com	$8 market orders; $13 limit orders; unlimited shares	6 a.m. to 10 p.m. EST weekdays	100 free quotes plus 100 for each order
Quick & Reilly	www.quick-reilly.com	$14.95 market orders; $19.95 limit orders; up to 5,000 shares	24 hours a day 7 days a week	100 free and 100 per order and unlimited for $29.95 a month

TABLE 3-2 *(Continued)*

Firm	Address	Online Price	Phone Help	Real-Time Quotes
Datek Online	www.datek.com	$9.99 up to 5,000 shares	8 a.m. to 7 p.m. EST weekdays	Unlimited free quotes
Suretrade	www.suretrade.com	$7.95 up to 5,000 shares	7 a.m. to 6 p.m. EST weekdays	100 free a day and 1 per order, unlimited for $29.95 a month
Discover Brokerage Direct	www.dbdirect.com	$14.95 market orders; $19.95 limit orders; up to 5,000 shares	24 hours a day 7 days a week	Unlimited free quotes
Dreyfus Brokerage Services	www.edreyfus.com	$15 for unlimited shares	9 a.m. to 7 p.m. EST weekdays	100 free and 100 per order and unlimited
National Discount Brokers	www.ndb.com	$14.75 market orders; $19.75 limit orders	7 a.m. to 8:30 p.m. EST weekdays	100 free quotes plus 100 for each order

*Applies only for customers making at least 12 trades a year.

Data as of December 1998.

RESEARCH TIP

For lists of available ADRs, research data, and other information, go to the premier ADR Web site at www.adr.com.

One easy way to buy ADRs is by using those aforementioned DRIPs. More than 100 are available as "no-load stocks" for $1,000 or less. U.S. investors can also purchase shares of foreign companies that are not listed as ADRs on U.S. stock exchanges. Just about any of the large brokerage houses can purchase stocks from Germany to Taiwan with a simple phone call. Of course, there are usually much higher trading costs concomitant with such orders.

Beware of Currency Risk

Whether you choose to buy your international stocks directly or through mutual funds, you run the additional risk of currency fluctuation. Foreign stocks are, of course, valued in their home country's currency—yen (Japan), pounds (England), pesos (Mexico), and so forth. Due to economic growth, inflation, and a host of other factors, the value of foreign currencies is constantly changing in relation to the U.S. dollar.

Mutual fund managers and other professional investors often use a complex process called "hedging" to protect their foreign investments against a sudden plunge in the currency value of the country where they own stocks (and bonds). Think of hedging as a form of portfolio insurance—it means that investors receive the full value of the changes in their overseas investments in dollars, minus the annual cost (usually less than 2% of the total) to hedge.

Many international fund managers argue that currency shifts "wash out" over several years and that the cost of hedging is too high. Thus they refuse to protect (insure) their investments against declining values of foreign currency. (See Chapter 7, where Mark Yockey, manager of Artisan International, makes exactly that argument.) Some international fund managers routinely hedge their whole portfolios, while others try to make currency predictions—hedging when they expect the dollar to strengthen and ending their hedges if they expect the dollar to fall.

U.S. tourists love a strong, muscular dollar. Its bulk means that foreign currencies are weaker, enabling them to travel more cheaply abroad. On the other hand, U.S. investors in international stocks love a weak, puny buck. It means a foreign corporation's earnings (and resulting stock price) translate into higher values whenever they are converted to U.S. dollars.

U.S. investors in international stocks in Asia, Africa, Russia, and Latin America suffered huge losses in 1998 as those stock markets fell dramatically in value. However, as the dollar rose dramatically against the ever-weaker foreign currencies, the losses were much worse for U.S. investors than for native investors in those countries. Let us illustrate:

1. A U.S. investor buys 100 shares of foreign company TUV at $10 per share.
2. The price of TUV stocks drops to $6.00 (a 40% decline).
3. The currency in TUV's home country falls 30% against the U.S. dollar.
4. TUV is now worth $4.20 in U.S. dollars (30% × $6.00 = $1.80 and $6.00 − $1.80 = $4.20).
5. The U.S. investor lost 58% of his or her investment ($10.00 − $5.80 = $4.20, or a 58% loss); the home country investor (or a foreigner who had completely hedged) lost only the 40% that the stock actually dropped.

Certainly the same scenario outlined above could (and did) happen to mutual fund managers. However, given their ability to hedge currency and, even more important, the diversification advantages that come from holding a large number of stocks from many different countries, such an outcome is far less likely. We believe that most investors, particularly the primary audience for this book—beginning and intermediate investors—are best served by confining their international investments to mutual funds (open-end and closed-end) as we do, unless they choose blue-chip foreign stocks (Sony, Royal Dutch Shell, etc.) listed as ADRs on U.S. stock exchanges.

Buying Hot Stocks and IPOs

Making really big money with sector investing is definitely possible. Certain sectors can simply catch fire from time to time, lifting just about every stock in that hot group to exorbitant valuations. Participating in such moves requires thoughtful foresight mingled with a dash of luck.

Certainly, 1998 featured the Internet stocks as its hottest sector. It seemed everything even vaguely related to the Internet went straight up. For example, during Thanksgiving week of 1998, in only four days of trading, Books-A-Million *moved up more than 1200 percent* as it sky-rocketed from $3^1/16$ to $38^{15}/16$ after announcing an enhanced Web site. Many privately held companies capitalized on the lust for all things Internet in 1998 by taking their companies public through IPOs.

The process of an initial public offering (IPO) begins when a privately held company decides to make its stock available to the general public for the first time. Under most circumstances, a private company will work with a large brokerage house that sponsors the IPO. After a fair price is determined (usually between $10 and $20 a share), the stock is listed on one of the stock exchanges and begins public trading for the first time.

uBid specializes in online auctions and offers just one example of several Internet-related IPOs in 1998. The stock came public at an initial offering price of $15 a share, with the first NASDAQ trade of $34^1/8$ a share at 10:30 a.m. The stock immediately shot up to $60, then dropped to $50, went back up to $58, and back down to $50—all within the first hour of trading. uBid

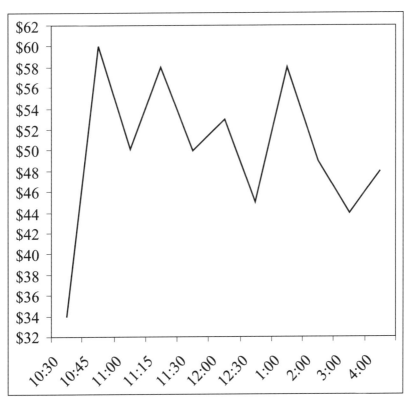

FIGURE 3-1   uBid's First Day (December 4, 1998)

TABLE 3-3   uBid's Closing Quote for First Day of Trading: December 4, 1998

uBID			
Last	48	Open	40
Change	+33	Previous close	15
% Change	+220.00%	Bid	47 1/4
Volume	9.124 Mil	Ask	47 1/2
Day's high	60 1/2	52-Week high	NA
Day's low	34 1/8	52-Week low	NA

According to a study by Jay Ritter, professor of finance at the University of Florida, most IPOs fail to perform as well as comparable, established companies in the same sector. Over a five-year period, established companies' stock generally outperformed the comparable IPO stock by 30%.

continued its wild ride, hitting a low of $44 before settling back to close at $48. So had just 100 shares been bought at the opening, a profit of as much as $2,500 could have been realized in less than 15 minutes. (See Figure 3-1.) And uBid didn't stop there. It eventually hit $189 a share before closing the year at $106^5/8$. The volatility of IPOs is often accentuated by the relatively few shares made available to the public; insiders often hang on to more shares than are traded. In uBid's case, there were roughly 1.5 million outstanding shares, but Table 3-3 shows the volume at over 9 million. That means each share was traded an average of six times on uBid's first day of trading.

It should be noted here that the general public can rarely buy hot IPOs at the initial offering price. The sponsoring brokerage house generally sells large blocks of shares to institutional investors and favored clients before the stock opens for trading on its particular stock exchange. Thus, in the case of uBid, the average investor was unable to purchase the IPO at $15, but rather had to wait until it opened at $34^1/8$ on the NASDAQ.

So big money can indeed be made in a very short amount of time by playing these hot IPOs. But money can also be lost—particularly when combined with playing golf. Golf alone can be an expensive sport. One short round of golf, in the late spring of 1996, cost over $3,000. It's a painful personal example.

We bought 100 shares of Excel Communications at $31 a share in May of 1996, a few days after it opened for public trading. We knew people who were involved with this relatively young provider of long-distance services and there was quite a buzz surrounding the stock. Our plan was to get in, make a small profit, and get out. The big run ensued over the next few days in late May. The stock hit $45 and we bought another 100 shares. That afternoon, the stock continued to climb to $51 and a quick nine holes of golf seemed a just reward for our insightful purchases. That evening, we discovered the stock had hit $56 a share before selling off in the last hour of trading, closing at an unbelievably low $34! So nine holes of golf cost more than $3,000 in lost profits. That's an expensive round of golf. Actually, we sold out a couple of days later at close to $38, just about breaking even for our efforts. And although we are big believers in the future of the telecommunications sector, Excel Communications traded at $22 a share late in 1998, $9 less (and two and one-half years later) than our original purchase price. The point: IPOs are extremely volatile and very risky. Let the buyer beware.

Market Orders

The above-described fiasco with Excel Communications could have easily been avoided with various types of stock orders. Specifically, a stop order would have done the trick and protected those profits. Using stock orders, the investor employs different methods of buying and selling individual securities.

The most common type of stock order is a market order. With a market order, the investor buys or sells a stock at the market price. The market price is the price at which the stock is currently being traded at the time the market order is placed. A market order to buy requires immediate purchase at the lowest offering (ask) price, whereas a market order to sell mandates a sale at the current highest offering (bid) price.

Limit Orders

Limit orders allow an investor to set the price at which a desired trade will be executed. For instance, if IBM is trading at $160 a share, but the individual

> The difference between the ask price (the price at which a current shareholder is willing to sell) and the bid price (the price at which a potential investor is willing to buy) is called the "spread." It is this spread that pads the profits for deep-discount and full-service brokers alike.

investor wants to pay only $156 a share, a limit order is the answer. The order is placed to buy IBM if the stock drops $4 a share, to trade at $156. Of course, the danger with limit orders is that the individual security will never strike the specified price and will end up trading much higher, leaving the limit price and potential profits behind. Limit orders can be used in the same manner to sell stocks.

Limit orders come in two varieties. A "good for the day" order, whether to buy or to sell, will expire at the end of the same business day in which that order first took effect. A "good 'til canceled" order will not expire until it is canceled by the investor or, as is usually the case at brokerages, will automatically expire after a set time period, typically 60 or 90 days.

Stop Orders

Although stop orders can be used to buy, they are more commonly directives to sell. With a stop order to sell, a price is set below the current market price at which the security is to be sold. Once the stock trades at the set price, the stop order immediately becomes a market order and is then executed at the best prevailing price. If the price never dips to the lower price of the stop order, then the security will never be sold. Stop orders are a type of insurance against sudden dips. Had we used a stop order with the 1996 Excel Communications example above, we would have sold our position while we were on the golf course, thus avoiding the drastic drop during the last hour of trading. Stop orders are generally used for two primary reasons:

1. To curtail a loss.
2. To protect a profit.

Long Versus Short

Most nonprofessionals trade almost exclusively "long." Buying stocks long simply means that the investor is betting that the stock price is going to go up in the future. This is how most stocks are bought. Average Joe investor calls his stockbroker and says, "Get me 200 shares of Coca-Cola." The stock is then purchased and tucked away in Joe's portfolio for years of blissful growth. That is termed buying the stock "long."

Now no one wants to be short, right? Well, sometimes, being "short" can really pay off. When an investor shorts a stock, she makes a bet that the stock will go down in price. With a short sale, the stock is not actually purchased. Rather, the short seller "borrows" the stock and promises to deliver the stock to the other party involved (usually a broker) at some undetermined time in the future.

Sometimes a stock can run up wildly and seem incredibly overpriced. A sharp decline seems imminent and a short sale is in order. If the stock subsequently drops, the insightful investor pockets a pile of cash. Of course, if the stock goes up, the short seller must deliver the stock as promised and therefore must take a loss on the transaction.

Such was the case in the fall of 1998 with the Internet stocks. Many of these companies were yet to show any profits, but their stock prices just kept spinning upward, seemingly out of control. A short would have

---

A "short" illustration. Mary Short feels that Intel is overvalued at $60 a share and believes the price will eventually fall to $45. She decides to sell 100 shares short at $60 for a total sale of $6,000. A certificate for 100 shares of Intel must then be delivered to the buyer on the opposite side of the sale. Since Mary Short does not actually own the shares, she borrows them from the brokerage house with which she is doing business. At some time in the future, Mary must purchase 100 shares of Intel and return them to the brokerage house that loaned them.

If Intel subsequently falls to $45 when Mary Short actually purchases her shares, then she pockets a $1,500 profit, less commissions ($60 − $45 = $15 × 100 shares = $1,500). If, on the other hand, Intel rises to $100 a share before Mary buys, then she realizes a $4,000 loss, plus commissions ($60 − $100 = −$40 × 100 shares = −$4,000). Also note that any dividends paid while the stock is borrowed go to the brokerage firm that lent it, not to Mary. And since there is theoretically no ceiling price on how high a stock can go, trading short can lead to losses far greater than Mary's initial investment. On the other hand, the maximum Mary can lose buying a stock long is her original investment, plus commissions.

indeed seemed the right move in October. But in fact, these stocks moved even higher. Sometimes stocks can go up for quite a long time with very little basis for such moves. For this reason and others, shorts are high risk and generally best left to the professional trader.

P/E Ratios

Knowing how to buy stocks is vastly different from knowing which stocks to buy. A price-to-earnings (P/E) ratio is one of the key elements to be evaluated when deciding which stocks to purchase. And the key to understanding a P/E ratio is to ask yourself, "How much am I willing to pay for the stock I want to buy?" A beginning investor might think that a stock selling for $50 is 10 times more expensive than a $5 stock. Not true: actually share prices are totally arbitrary. Suppose the JKL company has 10 million shares outstanding at $50 each or 100 million shares trading at $5 each—either way, JKL is exactly the same company with a $500 million capitalization, usually called "market cap."

JKL's real worth is measured by its profitability: obviously the more profit per dollar invested, the greater the value JKL has. If JKL earned $25 million in 1998, it would have a P/E ratio of 20 ($500 million market cap ÷ $25 million = 20). From another vantage point, JKL earned 5% for its shareholders ($25 million ÷ $500 million = 5%), and 100% divided by 5% is 20. Even more simply stated: for every $1 invested in JKL, a nickel profit can be projected on the basis of JKL's results for the past 12 months.

At the end of 1998 the average P/E ratio for all U.S. stocks was about 25, but Coca-Cola was selling for 40 times earnings. (Divide the amount earned per share into the share price to calculate its P/E multiple.) While Coke was selling at 40 times earnings, Continental Airlines was 5 times cheaper at 8 times earnings. At the same time, Cisco Systems, often called the "backbone" of the Internet and one of our favorites, sold at a P/E of over 80, double Coke's value. The disparity in the value of the three companies indicates conventional market wisdom: (1) Cisco Systems will report enormous profit gains in the future, (2) Coke will continue its consistent profit growth, and (3) Continental is not likely to increase its profits.

P/Es are an excellent way to compare stocks—but which P/Es should we consider? The P/E ratios listed in the *Wall Street Journal* and other publications are always based on *past* earnings. However, all of us buy stock to get *future* gains! As a result, market professionals sometimes talk about P/Es based on estimated future earnings. And of course, P/Es are irrelevant to Amazon.com and most other pure Internet plays. Any company that has no profits has no P/E!

RESEARCH TIP

Each week *Barron's* publishes estimated company earnings for the current year and the following year.

Maximizing Tax Efficiency

When it comes to maximizing tax efficiency, stocks definitely have the edge over mutual funds. As we stated in Chapter 2, mutual funds must make capital gains distributions each year, and many of those distributions are taxed at ordinary income rates. Stocks, on the other hand, are taxed only when they're sold. Thus, unlike mutual fund investors who delegate their sell decisions to mutual fund managers, stock owners can control their capital gains taxes. Of course, all stock dividends are taxed at ordinary income rates. But investors can minimize taxes on dividends by purchasing stocks that pay little or no dividends. Intel, for instance, pays out only about .2% in dividends per year. So investors in Intel have almost total control over when and how much tax they will pay.

Currently, capital gains tax rates are tied to two factors: the amount of time an individual stock is held and the stockholder's tax bracket. Capital gains are generally referred to as either short term or long term. Profits from the sale of a stock that has been held for 12 months or less are known as short-term capital gains. Profits from the sale of a stock that has been held for more than 12 months are referred to as long-term capital gains. Short-term capital gains are taxed at ordinary income rates. Therefore, an investor in the 15% tax bracket would pay a 15% tax on the gain. Likewise, an investor in the 36% tax bracket would pay a 36% tax on any short-term capital gain.

Long-term capital gains rates are a bit more complex. The maximum tax on a long-term capital gain is 20%. So an investor in any federal income tax bracket of 28% or higher will pay only 20% tax on profits from the sale of a stock held more than 12 months. However, investors in the lowest tax bracket, 15%, pay only a 10% tax. Wait, there's more. For stocks held an extra long time, five years or more, the maximum tax rate

TABLE 3-4   Capital Gains Tax Rates

Holding Period	Federal Tax Bracket	Capital Gains Rate	Effective Year
1 year or less	All tax brackets	Ordinary income rate	Current
1 to 5 years	15%	10%	Current
	28% and above	20%	Current
5 years or more	15%	8%	2001
	28% and above	18%*	2006*

*For stocks purchased in 2001 and after.

on capital gains eventually decreases to 18% in the year 2006. For the lower, 15% tax bracket, that five-year holding rate decreases to 8% in the year 2001. Table 3-4 displays the current capital gains tax rates, as well as future reductions and required holding periods.

Using Professional Help

A word about using professional help. If you are not a do-it-yourself investor, or if you just need a little one-on-one help to get started, then it makes sense to seek the help of a financial professional. Typically, personal finance magazines such as *Kiplinger's, Money, Smart Money, Worth,* recommend hiring a fee-only financial/investment planner to help you chart your financial course. Normal fees range from $100 to $500 per meeting. Because they refuse to accept any payment from any financial product they recommend, fee-only planners are often perceived as more "objective," avoiding a "conflict of interest." When they advise on mutual funds, they usually recommend almost exclusively no-load mutual funds.

Professional help can also be accessed by listening to and learning from mutual fund managers as they are profiled and interviewed on radio and TV and in the print media. Part Two of this book features interviews with managers of our favorite funds in each of the seven sectors covered. We learned a lot from these interviews—we think you will too.

The Investor's Toolbox

Riding the Silicon Wave: Investing in Technology and Communications

"**B**eam me up, Scotty." With those immortal words from Captain James T. Kirk, countless *Star Trek* fans marveled over the possibility of molecular manipulation. In the 1960s, Gene Roddenberry's vision of the future was truly revolutionary. But looking back now, his vision of the future seems antiquated in many ways. As many of us watched hours of *Star Trek* reruns, doors that opened automatically and a handheld device that enabled wireless communication seemed to be nothing more than pure fantasy. Today, we take both for granted. Of course, the possibility of molecular manipulation faintly glimmers like a distant star. And we do not yet have warp speed in order to reach that star.

Beware of Brazil

Investing in technology is much the same as writing science fiction. Some things eventually develop and others continually hold future promise, but never deliver. Consider videophones. Their commonplace role in American society has been predicted since the dawn of the age of television.

Didn't Dick Tracy wear something similar on his wrist? The problem is that videophones have been strictly "Brazil." According to technology writer Ilan Greenburg, "That's what the diplomats call a place that has great potential and always will."* Like Brazil's economy and molecular manipulation, the future vision never arrives.

"Brazil" is also the problem with technology and the future. In the final analysis, everybody is guessing, even the so-called experts. A few years back, who would have imagined that the Internet would even have existed, let alone be an ever-increasing source of commerce? At the rate technology changes, it is nearly impossible to keep up with current trends and products, let alone forecast the future. Your task then, as a technology investor, is to get past all the speculation. You must filter out the hype, leaving a residue of sound information from which you can make more intelligent investment decisions (or at least better-educated guesses).

A Brief History

A defining catalyst for the technology industry occurred in 1971 when Intel engineers invented the microprocessor. Using this processor as the central brain of the computer, research and development companies and hobbyists alike built a handful of PC prototypes. From this inauspicious beginning, the PC industry has exploded into a huge market with revenues surpassing $200 billion a year. The evolutionary, or revolutionary, change is not only fascinating but also critical to separating the hype from reality in order to ascertain where the industry can go from here.

Introduced in 1975, the MITS Altair 8800 was the first PC to gain wide use. Two youngsters named Bill Gates and Paul Allen wrote the first software program for the computer, and Microsoft Corporation began. There was a problem, though. That first software program required a paper punch card and had to have instructions toggled into the computer.

The Apple II computer, introduced in 1977, was the first PC infused into the mass market. It came complete with a monitor, keyboard, and spreadsheet program that many financial professionals could use. The commercial PC market was born. It began to grow over the next four years as many PC vendors entered the market. Two of the better-known brands

---

*William H. Inman, "Beyond Brazil: How to Turn Technology's Unending Promise into Profits," *Bloomberg Personal Finance,* October 1998, p. 14.

of that era were the Commodore Amiga and Atari 800, both from now-defunct manufacturers. With this proliferation of PC makers came the problem of uniform technical standards. They didn't exist. Each computer had its own operating system, processor, and software programs.

All that changed in 1981 when International Business Machines Corporation produced a personal computer with specifications that other manufacturers could copy. IBM licensed its operating system from Microsoft and its microprocessor from Intel. Both companies were free to license their products to other manufacturers, and IBM clones soon followed. The baby PC industry began to flex its muscle and grew steadily over the next several years with improvements such as Intel's 386 processor, introduced in 1985.

The maturation of the industry began in 1991, when Microsoft launched Windows 3.1. Windows broke from the text-based design of DOS by featuring graphic icons easily manipulated by using the point-and-click mouse. In 1992, the first year after Windows 3.1 became available, PC shipments jumped 20% to 32.4 million worldwide compared with a 13.4% increase the prior year. PC shipments reached 50 million a year in 1994. Innovations such as CD-quality video and sound, as well as public access to the World Wide Web have continued to fuel growth in the industry. It is estimated that nearly 100 million PCs were shipped worldwide in 1998. Meanwhile, prices continue to plunge and performance continues to excel. (See Table 4-1.) Despite recent problems, many analysts predict that the industry will continue growing at roughly a 15% rate for several more years.

TABLE 4-I Comparing PC Performance: Past and Present

	The Old	The New
Machine (year)	IBM is first PC (1981)	Packard Bell 820 (1998)
Price	$5,000	$900
Processor	Intel 8088/4.77 megahertz	Cyrix MII/333 megahertz
Memory	16,000–256,000 bytes	64 million bytes
Storage	Two 160,000 byte floppy drives	4.3 billion bytes

Data Source: *The Wall Street Journal*, 11/16/98

Driving the growth in the PC industry is the continued expectation that Moore's Law will indeed hold true for at least another decade. Named after former Intel Corporation chairman Gordon Moore, Moore's Law states that computer power doubles every 18 months without any price increase.

Segments of the Sector

In order to filter technology's winning companies from the losers, it becomes necessary to organize them in different categories. While technology companies come in many varieties, for our purposes, these categories number seven:

1. **Software companies.** These firms design the programs that tell computers how to operate. Microsoft is a clear leader in this category. Other specialty players include Intuit, the maker of Quicken and other financial software, as well as Network Associates, famous for its antivirus and networking software.

2. **Internet companies.** The players in this arena profit (or hope to profit) from the meganetwork that connects the world, from Chile to the Sudan, and Russia to Idaho. Granted, this is a nebulous category, since every tech player seems to have a finger in the Internet pie to one degree or another. Company names include Yahoo! and America Online.

3. **Networking companies.** These firms supply the desperately needed infrastructure for the information superhighway as well as networks for big corporations. Leaders include Cisco Systems, Lucent, 3Com, and Ascend Communications.

4. **Workstations and server companies.** These businesses provide expensive machines that power the giant Internet. Sun Microsystems is the big name here.

RESEARCH TIP

The National Association of Investors Corporation (NAIC) is a not-for-profit, largely volunteer organization dedicated to investment education. It offers a direct purchase plan similar to DRIPs that allows

many tech companies to be purchased for as little as $50 a month. Cisco Systems and Microsoft are just two of many tech companies that do not offer DRIPs, yet can be purchased through NAIC. There is a $39 yearly membership fee and fees to use the stock service. Call 888 780-8400 or visit the NAIC Web site at www.better-investing.org.

5. **Semiconductor companies.** On the high end, Intel is the only name you really need to know. These companies make the tiny chips that run everything from Palm Pilots to the standard PC. Microprocessors are the brains of the computer and the low-end market is quite competitive.

6. **Telecom companies.** These folks manufacture communication devices of all types and also provide the networks that make dialing a friend in Australia a breeze. This rapidly growing industry includes familiar names such as AT&T, but the real action is in the wireless field, where Swedish telecommunications giant Ericsson and Finland's Nokia play.

7. **PC manufacturers.** The PC segment of the tech industry—composed of Compaq, Dell, Gateway, IBM, and many more—builds the gateway through which most of us enter the high-tech world.

We would be remiss if we did not break down the Internet companies even further and consider what might lead to their success. **Infrastructure** is the first key to Internet investing. As the popularity of the Internet multiplies, the thinner the bottleneck becomes, restricting access to the most-favored sites. That problem will only grow worse as more and more communication is digitalized. Companies like Motorola and Lucent are perhaps best poised to profit from the inevitable infrastructure buildup. The problem of the "last mile" is also an issue. The last mile involves connecting high-speed wires from existing cables on the street to both neighborhood homes and commercial businesses. The large cable TV companies and Denver-based Qwest seem to have an edge in this arena.

Sometimes selling "nuts and bolts" to a larger tech company is more profitable than selling directly to consumers. The Internet company involved in **enabling technologies** might provide the software used for Internet security or the voice-and-video transmission used for multimedia communications. VeriSign is an example of the former and Real Networks of the latter.

Portals, another category of Internet investing, include the names that we most readily accept as Internet companies—search engine companies such as InfoSeek, Yahoo!, and Lycos. All Web gazing must go through a portal, and advertising dollars and lucrative comarketing contracts will follow.

Finally, there are **retailers** all over the web. A key element that makes a company successful on the Internet is branding. It appears that companies with trusted recognizable brand names have an edge online. This would give the brand names additional leverage when competing for electronic commerce. Bookseller Amazon.com is a notable exception, having surpassed giant Barnes & Noble, which waited until 1998 before establishing an online presence. Though still in its infancy, Amazon.com has done a superior job of becoming a "name brand" in the public mind; its stock price was up 967% in 1998.

The Internet and Information

The Internet is undoubtedly the "mother lode" for technology investors. By the end of 1998, 1 million new Internet users per month were joining the Web revolution in the United States. As the twenty-first century dawns, there could be as many as 1 billion users worldwide. A new Web site comes online every 60 seconds, and 60% of all online users spend two hours or more per week on the Net. The sale of new computers now outpaces the sale of television sets. In less than 12 months, with E-Schwab, Charles Schwab opened more than 700,000 new accounts, helping jump its assets under management by $50 billion. But what is driving the unbridled frenzy? Simply stated: *information.* Information empowers. And a society empowered can accomplish unbelievable feats.

Playing the Swings

"Throttle up." Those words continue to haunt our collective national conscience as the last words spoken to the space shuttle *Challenger* crew on that excruciatingly horrifying afternoon of January 28, 1986. Our excitement over teacher Christa McAuliffe's historic flight instantly vanished as towers of smoke shot across that clear blue Florida sky. We suddenly became a nation in mourning. Our confidence in the brightest minds in the world shattered; we sat wondering why. Technology had let us down.

Certainly we do not want to trivialize the deaths of those nine brave *Challenger* astronauts; however, with all due respect, investing in technology is too much like that fateful day. You can go from the highest of highs to the lowest of lows in a very short time. "Mood swings," as Kevin Landis calls them later in this chapter, come with the technological territory. Just as you are ready to blast into the stratosphere, something unexpected can bring you plunging back to earth.

Flash forward now to October 29, 1998. "Godspeed, John Glenn." Those historic words uttered again speak volumes to technology's ability to rise from the wreckage of disaster to new and endless possibilities. Imagine taking a commercial flight to space just like John Glenn, or taking a tour of the international space station. Someday we will. Technology, by its very nature, produces previously unimaginable opportunities and new innovations. And with each new innovation comes new demand for technological goods and services.

Given the sentiment shifts and wild swings in the technology sector, the question then becomes: how do we profit from the inevitable volatility? One way is to take advantage of the buying opportunities that this volatility consistently produces. It is not uncommon for such giants as Intel and Cisco Systems to go "on sale" 30% or more below their previous high. This is the time to buy. Even for a large-company technology fund like T. Rowe Price Science and Technology, we would recommend waiting for a 15% pullback before investing. For a small-cap tech fund like Firsthand Technology Value, it might be wise to wait for a 20% sell-off before jumping in.

Trust us, these tech funds will sell off. For instance, Firsthand Technology Value fell from $29 a share in early July 1998 to just over $18 in early October. The good news for Technology Value investors was that the fund went almost straight up from there, closing at $30.59 on December 4, 1998. That is a 35% decline followed by a 65% spike in less than six months. Even investors who followed our advice and got in after a 20% decline from the 1998 high of about $32 would have invested at roughly $25.50 a share. And by December 4, that investment would have already increased just shy of 20%.

Deciding when to buy an individual small-company tech stock is anybody's guess. These small stocks, even of relatively solid companies, will drastically sell off from time to time. This creates one of two opportunities: (1) the opportunity to buy scads of stock at incredibly discounted prices or

(2) the "opportunity" to throw scads of money at a company's stock just before it becomes virtually worthless. Such is the nature of the beast.

You'll notice we have yet to provide "sell" guidelines for the technology sector. Most fund managers will tell you that the "sell" decision is far more difficult than the "buy" decision. And with the tech sector, just when you think it can't go any higher, it spurts up another 20%. An additional problem is that active traders can become "market timers" as they attempt to catch the peaks and valleys. Market timing is an investing approach that almost never works in the long run.

A better strategy, used by many average investors, is to sell part of one's position after a big run-up. So if Cisco Systems more than doubles in fewer than three months, as it did in 1998, the investor could sell half, thereby taking some profit. The investor could either wait for Cisco to dip again before buying additional shares or find another tech company selling at a lower valuation. We recently employed this very strategy. In early October 1998, we purchased 200 shares of Cisco Systems at $43. Barely two months later, we sold 100 shares at $95. We then took most of the proceeds and invested in two promising new funds from Janus: Global Life Sciences and Global Technology.

Obviously, playing the swings in the tech sector is not for everyone. It takes increased time and attention. But of all the sectors, technology offers the greatest "home run" opportunities. And the nice thing about well-diversified investing in the tech sector is that even if you buy in just before a 30% plunge, all you need is a little patience. It will come back. Become a long-term investor in a diversified technology portfolio; you won't be disappointed.

Expert Interview: Kevin Landis, Technology Value Fund

Kevin Landis' Technology Value fund rocketed to back-to-back 61% returns in its first two full years in 1995 and 1996. Since then, Firsthand Technology Value has experienced greater turbulence. But a strong showing in late 1998 and 1999 garnered the fund the number 1 five-year ranking of all mutual funds through May 31, 1999—averaging 43.9% annually. This experience with both moods of the technology market, plus his extensive "firsthand" knowledge of the industry, enables Mr. Landis to give us a learned perspective of the tech sector.

SNAPSHOT

Kevin Landis currently manages two Firsthand funds: Technology Innovators and Technology Leaders. He is also comanager of a third fund, Technology Value, with Ken Kam. Before cofounding Firsthand funds, Kevin served as new products marketing manager for S-MOS Systems, Inc. Prior to S-MOS, he was an analyst at Dataquest, a high-technology market research firm. Kevin has an MBA from Santa Clara University, and a BS in electrical engineering and computer sciences from the University of California at Berkeley.

STEVE: I know there have been huge changes in the technology industry over the last 20 years. Could you give us a brief overview of those changes?

KEVIN: The last 20 years have been a transition from the computer being sort of an oddity that really didn't work its way into everyday life into something that suddenly helped you, and then became something that was intertwined with your daily life. The most visible example, of course, is the personal computer. But all of the other computers around you that you don't see are very important as well, like your antilock braking system. These are equally important. Another example would be your home security system. Or a more intelligent heating system in your house that can monitor the temperature in different rooms and can keep a constant steady temperature throughout your house.

STEVE: So 20 years ago would be the late 1970s. And PCs were basically nonexistent. Is that right?

KEVIN: Well in the late 1970s, people had heard of Apple Computer, but they did not really know who Apple was. And IBM had not yet entered the PC market. It just manufactured computers that only did specific tasks, like payroll for large companies. Computers existed then, but they didn't really affect day-to-day life. It was a technology that certain entities owned, whether it was NASA or the IRS. Somebody else owned computers and tackled big jobs with them...

STEVE: ...But not the average consumer.

KEVIN: Right.

STEVE: What about the Internet? Obviously, it's a more recent phenomenon. How do you see it changing the face of technology in the future?

KEVIN: Now that you have cheap computers everywhere, it becomes more about information. How do you get it? How do you share it?

And how do you move it around? So what's got people excited about the Internet has nothing to do with computers and has everything to do with getting information. It turns out that computers are a great tool to get information and to sort through information, but the end goal is still information. Let's say you're going to take a biking trip through Tibet. You can find out everything you need to know before you go. That's about information. And the computer that does the best job getting the needed information is the one that does it most unobtrusively.

STEVE: Though I can understand the enthusiasm over the Internet, I have to wonder about the valuations of these Internet companies. They are astronomical. Is this enthusiasm justified or are these Internet companies in unrealistic territory?

KEVIN: The enthusiasm over the Internet is justified. I would say the valuations of the individual stocks is another question. One of the nice things about being a technology investor is that you don't have to buy every stock. You don't have to invest in every great company out there. You can understand which companies you like and why you like them, and then buy them when you think the price is attractive. So what we do is we take a look at those Internet stocks and say, "Everybody has bid these up, if not to the sky, pretty close to it." So we will try to find a less obvious type of Internet play.

STEVE: What are some of those less obvious plays?

KEVIN: I draw a four-tiered model. On the top tier, I place those companies that give you a reason to go to the Internet such as Yahoo! and Amazon. These are what people think of as Internet companies. The things that these companies have in common is that they cause traffic because they provide people with information. So they are really information companies.

STEVE: And those are the ones that are overvalued in your opinion?

KEVIN: Well, those are the obvious ones. And the obvious ones are hardly ever a great deal. Let's ask ourselves, though, when somebody like Yahoo! boasts that they're getting more and more page use, "What does that mean?" Well then, let's go down to the next tier. These are the people who own the networks that have to carry all of that traffic. If traffic keeps going up, then owning a network is a more and more valuable thing because it is a more scarce commodity, right? So who owns all of that network capacity? Big companies like AT&T, World Com, Quest, and Sprint. These are the companies that actually own the physical networks. Now you could buy any of those stocks. But those companies need to spend a lot just to keep upgrading their networks. They are a little bit like cable TV companies used to be. They're investing a lot of money just to keep growing. So their cash flow looks pretty sparse. Now who do they spend money on? Well when somebody like World Com or AT&T decides that they want to build up their network a little bit to accommodate all of this growing Internet traffic, they buy the equipment from yet another group of companies. This group contains the likes of Lucent and Cisco, as well as some other very fine networking companies. Those stocks are a little bit more fairly priced, but they are still kind of expensive. So let's step down one more tier and ask, "Who are the suppliers to those companies? Who are the companies that are supplying the basic technology?" That is where I come up with my core group of investments in this sector. Specifically, they are chip companies who sell key technologies to people like Lucent and Cisco and Nortel and all of the other networkers. And those are companies such as PMC Sierra, Level One, Viatesse, and AMCC. These are some of our favorite picks, because they benefit from an increase in Internet traffic. They have a lot of Internet exposure, but they are just far enough removed so that it is not obvious to people what is going on. And because they are not so obvious, they are priced much more attractively.

STEVE: During the summer and early fall of 1998, the Russell 2000 performed poorly. But small-cap technology stocks did even worse.

KEVIN: They took a beating.

STEVE: What happened?

KEVIN: Investors are notoriously skittish when it comes to high-tech stocks. It is easy to feel like you are not entirely sure of what you own. If a company surprises you with bad news, then you can feel like they are a lot riskier than you thought. So there are times that due to market movements, people are afraid to own technology stocks.

STEVE: And one of those times was this last few months.

KEVIN: Absolutely. Now in this last month [November 1998] you have had the other fear. People think, "Technology equals growth," and they are afraid that they will be left out of that growth.

STEVE: We also call that greed. Is this volatility, then, something that simply must be embraced or is there a way to mitigate the volatility?

KEVIN: I think you can count on the mood swings in the marketplace as long as you are investing in high-tech. I think these swings are just a fact of life. If that is a show stopper for you, then you are not going to be a high-tech investor. In fact, you should not be a high-tech investor, because if you can't stomach that volatility, then what will happen is that you will end up getting out on the dips. And selling out on the dips is one of the few ways that you lose money investing in a growth industry.

STEVE: Other than those Internet plays, what parts of technology do you see as being successful going forward?

KEVIN: In the near term, it is all about bandwidth—the ability to move more information. It is not just the Internet, although the Internet is a great driver for bandwidth. It can also be wireless technologies, which have really taken a beating this year and look poised to have a great 1999. Another area that should be successful to some extent is the more classic high-tech industry. These companies simply profit based on trends in computing such as enterprise software or even occasionally the PC market.

STEVE: John Glenn just reentered space at 77 years of age. And the way NASA plans to do business in the future includes the use of many private companies. What's out there for technology? What changes do you see on the horizon?

KEVIN: Well, if we are talking about space, it is clear that the satellite business is very much a commercial business now. It is very much about getting payload into orbit efficiently. Just ask the Iridium folks who lost a couple of satellites on the way up whether the money really matters there. So I think that what will happen is some of these great minds that have been dedicated to defense are now going to be dedicated to the business of satellites. And that has great implications for having that Iridium idea eventually become a reality—the idea that you can walk all round the planet with a cell phone and hook up just about any place.

STEVE: What, then, is your outlook for global telecommunications?

KEVIN: You are going to see a combination of technologies. You are going to see fiber-optic technologies really taking over the high-capacity backbone parts of the network. You'll see wireless communication going into a lot of Third World areas where the terrain is perhaps a little bit rugged. You'll see satellite as sort of the mortar that fills in around the bricks. So if you are in an area that is lightly populated or that does not have another kind of service, you can always fall back on your satellite network. I think that one way the planet will be different when you are talking to your grandchildren is that you will have to explain to them that there were times when people really were isolated. And you will have to explain what it meant to be isolated and not know who had just won the World Cup, or not know that John Glenn had just been lifted into space.

STEVE: So this global telecommunications revolution will indeed affect even the most remote parts of the world.

KEVIN: I think so. In terms of whether that happens 5 years from now or 15 years from now—that all depends on the macroeconomic factors. And kind of going hand in hand with that thought, for the United States, is the idea that high-tech becomes more and more about exporting the high value-added part of the business.

STEVE: Which is…?

KEVIN: …Which is not necessarily the manufacturing, but the design and engineering of communications and computing gear and all the information technologies.

STEVE: Are you excited about the prospects for the telecommunications companies like Nokia or do you just buy the companies that supply components to the Nokias of the world?

KEVIN: I will play them both. I think the people who were going to make their money last year and this year in the Far East are having a hard time right now. But to me, those hard times just represent the entry points. I think that eventually we will get back on the road to hooking up the entire planet.

STEVE: One more question on telecommunications: how do you view the Baby Bells like Ameritech? Do you see them mostly as a utility or a technology company?

KEVIN: Oh, I think that they are purely a tech company. They offer communications services, but they are basically an information and a connectivity vendor. They will buy pieces of technology and they will integrate them and provide them. So I would not consider the phone industry as a utility. I think that whole group has been shaken up pretty fast and pretty hard. People like Ameritech, and I am not an expert on Ameritech—but people who come out of the Baby Bells are being outflanked every day by the younger, faster, and nimbler companies that don't act like they are monopolies. And if the Baby Bells continue to act like they are Baby Bells, then they will become less and less important as time goes along.

STEVE: With these rapid changes that we have been discussing in the technology industry, does it become practically impossible for the individual investor to play the smaller tech companies that you buy? Should the individual simply stick to Microsoft, Dell, and Cisco and leave it at that?

KEVIN: It depends on the investor's background. I believe in investing in what you know and investing in what you understand. So if that investor knows a company pretty well and knows why they like that company, then there is no reason why an investor should not be able to invest in it. But individual investors also have the luxury of being able to buy a few individual stocks and then going out and buying a fund....The thing that I encourage individual investors to do is go ahead and buy their favorite stocks on their own if they have that urge. But when you look for diversification and look to get your money generally employed into tech—that is what a mutual fund is for.

STEVE: Technology is obviously here to stay. We won't be going back to those 1970s computers. But are there other, more subtle reasons to invest specifically in the technology sector?

KEVIN: I think that you can start with the macro question. And that is: "What do I think is going to grow?" Because if you want to invest for growth over the long term, it is best to have the wind at your back. Technology is a growth business and it will remain a growth business probably for the rest of our lives. So I think that most investors want to have exposure to that growth. Now because technology companies are constantly doing different things, there are lots of unknowns out there. There will be some unknown disappointments and there will be some unknown pleasant surprises. And you are going to be exposed to both kinds of surprises. So as long as you know that the volatility in mood swings around these stocks is part of the package and you are willing to have the discipline to accept that in order to participate in the growth, then whatever portion of your investments that you want to have grow over a long period of time should be invested in technology or other industries with that kind of a profile. Invest in those industries with a real good long-term potential for growth.

STEVE: Your Technology Value fund had back-to-back 61% returns in 1995 and 1996 before coming back to reality in 1997. Obviously, 61% is not a realistic expectation for returns. What do you feel can be reasonably expected from technology over the next five to seven years?

KEVIN: I would say that historically the market returns somewhere in the teens. Around that number, some years are good and some years are bad. So there is a lot of variation in returns. Historically, high-tech returns better than the market. I don't know if it's twice what the market does or one and a half times what the market does. But if you go back and look at the numbers, high-tech does better than the market because high-tech is growth. Then you simply look at the peer group of high-tech mutual funds and pick one. Even if you pick a lousy high-tech fund relative to its peer group, you might still do better than if you picked an excellent general equities fund, just because high-tech was so strong.

STEVE: ...Over time.

KEVIN: Yes.

STEVE: Before we wrap up, could you give us your outlook for medical technology?

KEVIN: I can just give you some broad brushstrokes. Medical technology shares with high-tech the fact that there are more smart people working in it than ever before. And those smart people have better tools and better access to information than they have ever had before. So it is reasonable to expect great things from them given time. Meanwhile, the population is aging. So it is good that they are coming up with a great things, because we need it more and more. And if you look around, whether it is pacemakers or advanced treatments of cancer or things like arthroscopic surgery for your knee, you'll see that we have come a long way in the past few decades and there are a lot more great advances on the horizon.

STEVE: Any other major dangers or risks for the technology investor to be aware of?

KEVIN: I would say that for an individual investor the number 1 risk investing in high-tech is liquidity. By that I mean putting your money in as a long-term investment and then needing that money sooner than you thought. That circumstance, combined with the uncomfortable feeling that the ups and downs can give you is what can cause you to trade out at just the wrong time. So when you are making that decision about how much money to put into high-tech, you need to assume the worst, because there are going to be times that feel that way. And you need to know that in those volatile times you have not invested so much money into tech that you feel like you need to pull some money back out. Because that is one way you will hurt your chances for successful technology investing.

STEVE: Those are good words. Thank you.

Country songbird Shania Twain hopes someone will come on over and purchase her plush Adirondack estate, on the market for $7.5 million. The 3,000-acre spread near Lake Placid, N.Y., has five bedrooms, five bathrooms and a three-story recording studio. And if, as the song goes, that don't impress you much, maybe the heated nine-stall stable, tennis court, private lake or breathtaking views of Cat Mountain will do the trick. Shania and her husband, music producer Mutt Lange (who bought the place for $1.2 million in 1993), still own retreats in Florida and Switzerland where, of course, the twain shall meet.

MERRILL L. THOMAS INC.

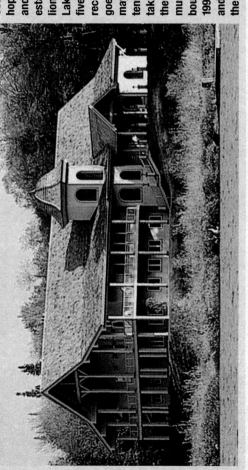

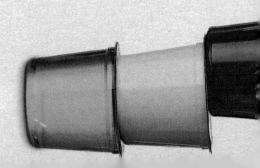

I could go for something

JELL-O
BRAND
®

www.jell-o.com

CHAPTER 5

Saving with the Baby Boomers: Investing in Financial Services

Shh....Make sure no one is looking over your shoulder. It's time for a secret. Suppose at the beginning of 1996, you had perfect foresight. You picked the very best fund from each of the three largest publicly traded mutual fund families: Franklin/Templeton, Merrill Lynch, and T. Rowe Price. Perfect! You hit the Trifecta for an average annual return of 26.2% from 1996 to 1998. What could be much better? Well, let's suppose that, instead of purchasing the best mutual fund from each of the three, you decided to buy the stocks of these three fund companies. Wow! You hit the jackpot with a 35.6% three-year average annual return. By owning the fund companies themselves, you would have profited $14,933 on an initial investment of $10,000 versus a gain of $10,099 from purchasing each company's number 1 fund. (See Table 5-1.)

Increased Profits

So now you know! Instead of sorting through hundreds of mutual funds from fund giants Franklin/Templeton, Merrill Lynch, and T. Rowe Price to

TABLE 5-1   1996–1998

Fund Family's Stock Performance		Fund Family's Best Mutual Fund	
Franklin/Templeton	24.6%	Dynatech I	23.4%
Merrill Lynch	39.9%	Fundamental Growth B	27.1%
T. Rowe Price	42.4%	Blue Chip Growth	28.1%
Average	35.6%		26.2%

find their star fund winners, you could have made a far more rewarding decision to simply purchase their stocks. Why have the stocks of mutual fund companies (and, to a lesser extent, other financial services companies) done so well during the 1990s?

Mutual fund companies have experienced tremendous growth because millions of Americans now use mutual funds in 401(k)s and other pension plans as their primary long-term savings choice. For example, more than 80% of Fidelity's $90 billion Magellan fund is in tax-sheltered plans. Yet mutual fund expense ratios now average 1.35% annually, 27% higher than at the end of 1983. Given the great bull market of the past 15 years, most investors have virtually ignored costs, focusing instead on performance. Therefore, most mutual fund companies have not chosen to pass on their economies-of-scale lower costs to their customers. As a result, profits have soared, sending the shares of publicly traded mutual funds higher and higher.

Banks too have found ways to increase profit margins by raising fees. The examples seem almost endless: ever-increasing ATM surcharges, numerous check writing and cashing fees, high credit card rates and late penalties, higher bounced-check fees, and so on. Some banks even charge a fee to talk personally with bank tellers. And while all these charges are annoying to many bank patrons, their cumulative effect adds to shareholder value.

Another factor driving the increase in profitability for fund companies and other financial services firms is simple demographics. Typically, most Americans don't become serious about saving until their mid-forties. For example, the older coauthor of this book threw away his yearly pension report until 1983; at the age of 47 he decided he ought to keep the annual statements to see if he could "afford to retire" someday. And many of today's 76 million baby boomers, born from 1946 to 1964, are asking the same question. The built-in demand for financial services as they approach their peak earnings *and savings* years is extremely powerful.

Demographics and higher fees only offer a partial explanation for the terrific returns to investors in financial service companies since the late 1980s. Many were due for a natural rebound. Financial firms were often out of favor in the mid-1980s when the U.S. government took over numerous banks and savings and loans, particularly in Texas, California, Arizona, and Florida, where weak state regulation combined with lax national standards to eventually force taxpayer bailouts for depositors. This savings and loan fiasco pushed many financial stocks lower and paved the way for a good run in the 1990s. In addition to the bounce-back from their misery in the 1980s, financial services have benefited and continue to benefit from a technology revolution and a merger wave—both combine to slash payroll costs and boost profits. Finally, lower interest rates and a strong economy are also particularly buoying for financial services stocks.

The Consolidation Game

Consolidation is a recurrent theme as banks and other financial services companies announce continual mergers and buyouts. Two of the biggest mergers in 1998 were between Travelers/Citibank and Nations Bank/Bank of America. David Ellison, manager of FBR Financial Services and Small Cap Financial Services, thinks that investors should not get caught up in trying to guess which bank is a likely takeover prospect (see his interview below). Many of these potential bank buyout targets may be overpriced; in effect, a takeover premium is already reflected in their share prices. Ellison argues that investors will do best by focusing on banks that are likely to be buyers, not sellers.

Buying Small Banks

With virtual online banking a reality and with the continuing banking consolidation among larger banks, it may surprise you to learn that 1998 set an all-time record for the creation of new, small, community banks. As the bigger banks merge, they downsize by cutting high-paid executives. Thus, they create a talent pool of local entrepreneurs who believe that bigger is definitely not better. The Jimmy Stewart, *It's a Wonderful Life* appeal of a caring, locally owned, community bank is still extremely powerful. Prior to 1998, most of these small-bank start-ups had done exceptionally well.

By far the best way to make a quick profit on small-bank stocks is to buy the initial shares (IPOs) offered by a local savings and loan (S&L) as it converts from a mutual thrift (owned by its depositors) to a publicly traded corporation (owned by investors). Eligibility to buy shares at the IPO price, usually $10, $12, or $15, is established by being a customer of the thrift. Typically, savvy investors deposit as little as $500 to $1,000 in a CD at S&Ls they suspect are likely to convert. If the conversion takes place, they receive a letter offering them the chance to buy a limited number of IPO shares.

According to a December 1998 article in *Kiplinger's Personal Finance Magazine,* 92% of the savings and thrifts that have gone public since 1992 were higher than their opening prices a month after their IPOs. Their stock appreciation can be quite astounding. We met a man in 1993 who had bought the most IPO shares in 1990 that his thrift would permit—$200,000 worth. After the thrift's conversion and subsequent buyout by a bigger bank, his $200,000 initial investment in 1990 grew to more than $900,000 within three and one-half years.

Buying Large Institutions

If buying a small local bank or a bank IPO doesn't appeal to you, consider buying individual direct DRIPs: Mellon Bank (owner of Dreyfus mutual funds) and Regions Financial, a regional Alabama-headquartered bank, are two possibilities. We own John Hancock Bank and Thrift Opportunity fund (BTO), a highly rated closed-end fund that should be considered for purchase whenever it sells for a 10% discount or more to NAV. For no-load mutual fund investors, we like both FBR funds managed by David Ellison, FBR Financial Services, and Small-Cap Financial. Or check out Price Financial Services (available for as little as $50 monthly).

In addition to the stocks of the three mutual fund giants we spotlighted at the beginning of this chapter, there is another publicly traded brokerage/mutual fund giant, Morgan, Stanley, Dean Witter, that may do quite well. It's also available for a minimum purchase of $1,000 as a direct DRIP. Unfortunately, Fidelity, the largest mutual fund company, is privately owned and Vanguard, the second largest, is a nonprofit, owned by its investors.

We have a well-capitalized and very successful mutual thrift, Piedmont Savings and Loan, in our hometown of Winston-Salem, NC. It constantly receives inquiries and even checks from out-of-state investors wanting to open accounts. It routinely denies all out-of-state requests and carefully screens applicants who do not live in nearby North Carolina counties. It has been rumored for several years that Piedmont has "plans to go public" but its executives consistently say no.

Buying Insurance Stocks

Finally, we would be remiss if we did not highlight insurance stocks. The consolidation in the insurance industry is at an early stage, lagging the merger frenzy in banking. However, almost all insurance stock analysts are predicting fewer and fewer insurance companies in the next decade as buyouts multiply. One top mutual fund manager, Scott Satterwhite of Artisan Small Cap Value, recommends buying small insurance companies that are dominant in their niche. We own two of his picks: a reinsurance company in Bermuda (ALRE) and a crop insurance company in the Midwest (AIF).

Two well-managed insurance giants can be purchased without commissions via the DRIP route. Both Allstate and Equitable may be purchased for as little as $500. One fine no-load fund, Century Shares, specializes in buying almost all insurance stocks.

Expert Interview: David Ellison, FBR Small Cap Financial Services

David Ellison is a very focused man. He buys only U.S. financial stocks. And he does it well. You will definitely profit from his insights.

SNAPSHOT

David Ellison joined FBR following a successful career with Fidelity Investments, where he managed the Fidelity Select Home Finance fund from its 1985 inception until September 1996. When he resigned from Fidelity, David had the number 1 rating of any U.S. fund manager at the same fund for 10 years. He manages two FBR funds—the Small Cap Financial fund and the larger-cap Financial Services fund. He has a BA in economics and English from St. Lawrence University and earned a MBA from Rochester Institute of Technology in 1983.

STEVE: Can you give us a brief history or overview of the financial sector and what's been driving the industry over the past several years?

DAVID: If you go back to let's say the 1988 to 1992 period...

STEVE: ...To the savings and loan crisis.

DAVID: Right. There was a severe credit crunch and a severe real estate recession. That really set us up for the legislative reorganization of the insurance funds. In a sense, it was a resetting of the clock in terms of the regulatory environment. And that has been the framework under which we have been working since 1990. We've had a much stronger regulatory framework due to all these troubles. Obviously, most of the companies didn't fail and there was a significant improvement in non-performers. This has gotten us where we are today in terms of improved earnings and higher stock prices. We are reaping the fruits of better regulation. Obviously, credit conditions today are still quite good.

STEVE: So was that the key to the improved performance in the financial sector: a stabilized regulatory environment?

DAVID: I think the improvement in performance was really due to two things. One, it was the improvement in asset quality that really started in 1990 and 1991. That combined with the second factor: a much stronger regulatory regime in response to what happened with the Bank of New England failure and the record number of other failures. This all created an awareness on the part of the regulators and the legislative people to really stiffen up everything. And that in turn created a much better backdrop for the banks and thrifts. The market then became convinced that they were much more strongly and adequately regulated.

STEVE: That's interesting. In this case regulation actually helped.

DAVID: It definitely did. I first started looking at this industry in the early 1980s. The regulators then were basically friends of the banks and thrifts. They went along with whatever the industry did. They bent the rules and changed the accounting schemes. And they were really an ally to the banks and thrifts and insurance companies. This cozy relationship created a lot of problems due to bipartisan legislation and bipartisan action on the part of the regulators. That eventually backfired, because the industry took it to the logical extreme and abused the system.

STEVE: Some people argue that the financial sector's high returns of the last decade are over and that continued outperformance is an unrealistic expectation.

DAVID: I think that every investor should think about that no matter what part of the cycle we're in. The question is: what are the companies doing to try to compete more effectively and what are they doing on a quarterly basis to improve the operations of the company? That is what I have always tried to focus on. I can sit here and talk to you like we just did about the broad reasons as to why the stocks did well. But at the end of the day, it was really a quarter-by-quarter examination of earnings. If earnings continue to do reasonably well, then the stocks will follow.

STEVE: Then you see earnings as the key factor to the sector and not the broader, macro questions?

DAVID: Obviously, other factors affect earnings. You really have four things that drive the industry. Those four things are (1) interest rates, (2) credit quality, (3) regulatory changes, and (4) accounting changes or adjustments.

STEVE: What about the megamergers? We've seen Travelers come together with Citicorp. Will this continue or are there other systemic changes on the horizon?

DAVID: Well, I think there is always going to be consolidation at least as long as I am alive. There are enough companies out there for mergers to continue. There are about 2000 thrifts and 4000 banks. I don't know what the exact numbers are. It is hard to keep up with it because things change so much. There's also, for example, a record number of new bank charter applications pending today. Obviously, the little ones are insignificant. But in terms of the number of banks and thrifts, people look at it and say, "That is an absolute number and it is always going to decline." That is not true.

But the question was: what about these big guys? I'm not convinced that bigger is always better. There is no economic or statistical proof historically that bigger banks outperform smaller banks on an ROE [return on equity] or an ROA [return on assets] basis. If anything, it is just the opposite. So as an investor, I am not saying to myself, "I have to own all of the big names because that is where the excess returns are." My belief is that the excess returns are in the midcap or small-cap names.

STEVE: You've talked about this proliferation of small banks. Is it a good idea for the average person to buy stock in a neighborhood bank, especially when it first goes public?

DAVID: Based on what is happening in the market today, most of these stocks sell at a premium on their first day of public trading. Yet I don't think that I have seen a deal that has actually gone down in eight years. So from that point of view, it is a sign of the market and a sign of where they are priced. Buying in is fine if you choose a reasonably well-managed small hometown bank and you understand its market and it has been around for 50 or 60 years. Remember that when most of these smaller banks come public, they are not new companies. I own some companies that have just gone public but they have been around for 100 years.

STEVE: So you're saying as long as an investor has the feel for what that hometown bank is doing...

DAVID: Right. The important thing when you look at these smaller companies is the local market that they're in and what they are trying to accomplish. The banking business is not a new business. Loans have been made for 500 years. You can go back to the Bank of England. People have been making loans, and they have been taking deposits. They have been making unsecured loans. They call them credit cards now. Back then, there were loans on ships going across the ocean. Banking plays off interest rate risk, credit risk, and inflows of capital and has been going on for a long, long time. It is one of the oldest industries around.

STEVE: So for those trying to get a handle on the business today, what are your particular criteria for valuing a stock? And is there a difference between important criteria for a small bank versus a large one?

DAVID: When you talk about the small company, what is really important is looking at the management's ability to currently run the bank and management's goals. If their goals are reasonable and they have a reasonable plan and that plan includes increasing earnings with a limited amount of risk, then that is a good deal. Plans are not usually that complicated. So if the bank is trying to make loans here, and trying to take deposits there—they are trying to buy branches here and trying to do acquisitions there—if it makes sense to you, then you should stay with it. But if it is something you do not understand where they are making loans 200 miles away on condominium projects that you have never seen or never heard of, then it is not worth buying the stock. Because I am sure that if you do not understand it, then the management does not understand it.

STEVE: What about the larger institutions? Are there different factors to consider when preparing to invest?

DAVID: Yes. I think with the big boys you worry more about what is happening on the macro level. Because these banks are bigger, they have more geographic dispersion. They have much more complicated balance sheets. It becomes a question of whether rates are going up or down and what is happening to credit quality. Because invariably the bigger institutions show the change in credit quality first. The little guys in their local markets will rarely make a bad loan. They understand their market so well and they are not going to make those crazy loans. With the bigger names, you have to be more focused on what is happening from a top-down point of view.

STEVE: With the smaller names, it is more bottom up.

DAVID: Right. The average investor can probably do better in the smaller names because he has a better feel for what's going on from the bottom up. And it is the same with me. That is why I have always favored the smaller names—because I do not like to bet on whether or not rates will fall and if the yield curve will expand. I do not know when that is going to happen. So I want to own somebody who is doing the blocking and tackling today and doesn't need to have rates move and doesn't need a change in government policy. Small banks do not need some variant from the federal government in order to do a deal, as was the case with Chase and Travelers.

STEVE: Plus, with small banks, they could possibly be bought out.

Yield curve is a term applied to a graph of the relationship between U.S. Treasury bonds of varying maturities and their yields. Bond maturities of three months, one year, ten years, and so on go along the x-axis while the percentage yield goes along the y-axis. Plot the yield of each maturity; connect the dots and presto! A yield curve appears. Plotted on a graph, the upward-sloping line is called a positive or "normal" yield curve. When short-, intermediate-, and long-term rates are the same or differ just slightly, the yield curve is said to be "flat," since the graph line is almost straight. However, even though it's unusual, it's possible to have an "inverted" yield curve when long-term rates are lower than short-term rates. (An inverted yield curve usually forecasts a recession.) Banks most often make their best profits when the yield curve is steeply positive. A steep yield curve enables banks to make higher profits by increasing their spreads; they can borrow short-term money cheaply from the Fed and then lend it at much higher rates long term to their customers.

DAVID: Maybe they get bought out and maybe they don't. But the important thing to do, and what I have always done, is to focus on the buyers and not the sellers. I don't want to have to depend on a buyout in order to make money. The buyouts can come and go very quickly. The idea is to always try to protect the downside. If the only reason you wanted this $20 million little thrift is: "Well it doesn't make any money but it will get bought out because the chairman is old or he is ill or his son doesn't want to be in the business." That's all garbage! What are you betting on? "Inside sources tell me…" It's garbage. Sometimes it works and sometimes it doesn't. It has worked quite well over the past year or so because everything has been getting bought out.

STEVE: We have talked a lot about buying a stock. What are your criteria for selling a particular stock?

DAVID: There are a couple of things. First, if management changes their plan and it doesn't make sense to me or I can't understand it, then I would sell. For example, a company goes from being a traditional mortgage lender to suddenly doing D-Prime auto paper (auto loans to very high credit risk individuals). I would say, "Wait a minute. You don't know anything about that." I'm not going to wait until you prove to me that you can do it before I sell. Invariably what happens is that they are not successful.

STEVE: Returns of 20% have spoiled many investors since 1995. What do you see as realistic returns for the financial sector for the next decade?

DAVID: As a benchmark, I have always told people that you have to look at the return on equity as an indicator of where the returns can be. The return on equity now is in the high teens. And I feel that a realistic return on equity is somewhere between 10% and 15%. That implies that the return you are likely to get going forward is going to be between 10% and 15%.

STEVE: That is quite a wide variance.

DAVID: There is a wide variance because this is to some degree a cyclical business. You have changes in interest rates and changes in credit cost and changes in loan volume. Right now we are seeing the higher end of the range because you have very little credit cost. You have high loan volume as indicated by record home sales and record vacancy rates in some cases in the commercial market. And then you also have reasonably good interest rates. You don't have any really big negatives out there right now. And as those negatives come in and are mitigated, the return on equity will tend to go to the lower end and then bounce back up again. I think we are at the higher end of the profit range at this point because of the favorable economy. The environment for the banks is not unlike it is for Microsoft or IBM or Home Depot for that matter.

STEVE: You have outlined some compelling reasons to invest in the financial sector.

DAVID: I think that the reason you own financial stocks is because, in the simplest sense, it is an industry that is still poorly run with poor efficiencies and below-average management.

STEVE: Still?

DAVID: I don't mean to offend anyone. But clearly, at the end of the day, the industry has its ups and downs and has suffered because of poor management both on the regulatory side and on the management side. I think one of the reasons you own this industry is because there is demand for the product. And it is always important to have demand for your product. That is shown in the fact that you have inflows into mutual funds and general demand for financial services products. I suspect that over the next 10 years you will have continuing improvement in management, which will lead to a more efficient operation. This industry is still overemployed. It still has too many bodies for the assets that it is managing and the products it is selling.

STEVE: So you think that profits could be increased simply by some cost-cutting measures?

DAVID: Oh yeah. You are going to have continued cost cutting. This is a long process. It is not going to happen overnight. And that is a another reason why I like this industry. Change happens slowly. From a fund management point of view, it is nice to have an event that is capitalized over a long period of time, as opposed to saying, "O.K. Citicorp is going to take an $18 billion charge, lay off a half the employees, and go from being an average company to an above-average company in like a month." Sometimes you see these big restructuring charges come out and all of a sudden the company is repaired. The problem is that it is all capitalized very quickly. Meaning the market recognizes it and bids the stock up in one day.

STEVE: So if you are not right there, you miss the big move.

DAVID: Right. What I am saying is that this is going to happen over a long period of time, which gives me a chance to own Citicorp or a Norwest or a Webster Financial for five or six years. I'd rather have a 15% or 20% stock per year than have an 80% rise in one day. The capital gains issue is no longer a major problem. You can then say you bought the stock six years ago at $20 and it is now $60. That makes a great story. You know it is not going from $20 to $80 like these Internet stocks, and then from $80 back to $20. I'd rather have a slow progression. So basically I think that you make most of your money in the market by owning companies that go from an average company to an above-average company, rather than from an above-average company to a great company. I think that the financial industry as a whole is still below average. Their expenses are too high and the regulatory environment, though improved, is still a burden. And they still have the wrong product mix. For example, banks still emphasize CDs and passbook savings rather than mutual funds and annuities. That mix is starting to change through consolidations like Citicorp and Travelers, and Melon and Dreyfus. Still, these changes are happening slowly.

STEVE: So what gives you such long-term confidence?

DAVID: We will have our ups and downs. There will be buying opportunities. The stocks are not going to go up forever. If the yield curve inverts and the economy goes into recession, then we are going to have credit troubles and were are going to have spread troubles. The stocks will go down because earnings will go down. And then at that point, the stocks will rally back. But I am in it for the long haul. I'm not a hedge fund manager that is trying to pick off some two-month trend. At this point in the cycle, I try to buy the best-run companies that are going to do well in a difficult environment.

STEVE: What about the Pacific Rim crisis? Is that a concern or are there other dangers of which we should be wary when investing in the financial sector?

DAVID: The danger always is getting into names where you do not understand how they make money. I do not own a J. P. Morgan. I do not own Bankers Trust. I don't think they are bad companies, but I cannot understand how they make money for more than an hour at a time. It doesn't mean I'm stupid. It doesn't mean they're stupid. It just means that I am not going to buy into companies I don't understand. The important thing that I say to investors is to stick with the companies that you know.

STEVE: And you stick mostly with banks?

DAVID: I have focused historically on banks and thrifts and life insurance companies. I don't like property and casualty companies because I am not a very good weatherman. These companies will say, "We had a bad winter in Detroit." Wait a minute. I missed that snowstorm in Detroit because I wasn't watching the weather channel every day. Or maybe there was excess heat in Texas. And it is always a negative. It is never, "Oh, we had great weather in that region, so therefore we had bigger gains." Or, "It was a nice night; therefore we made a couple of pennies extra per share." Also, the reason I focus on banks, thrifts, and life insurance companies is because they are the least best.

STEVE: They have the most room for improvement.

DAVID: Right. The mutual fund industry is already doing great. They have the lowest cost of capital. They have the lowest employee count per asset. They have the simplest regulatory framework to deal with. The mutual fund industry has done great for 10 years. Fidelity is there and I'm here. And I guess that you are in your business partly because of the growth in the mutual fund business.

STEVE: That's true.

DAVID: I'm not complaining about it. It is just a reality. But why buy into something that has already had such unbridled growth? It is an industry that already has all the right products. Remember, I want to buy into companies that are now below average, but moving to above average. And the same would hold true for the brokerage stocks. The brokerage stocks have had clear sailing for four or five years now. Again, it is one of those things where you are buying into an industry that has had a record harvest every year. 1988 was really the best time to buy those stocks. The underwritings were horrible. That was after the 1987 crash. I think the Bank America/Nations Bank deal is going to have about $600 billion in assets postdeal. And they will have about 180,000 employees combined. Fidelity has about $600 billion in assets and only has about 30,000 employees.

STEVE: How much more efficient can Fidelity get?

DAVID: It could get more efficient. But I've always believed in the three basic things of capitalism, which are land, labor, and capital. The banks have tons of labor. GM doesn't hold a candle to what the banks have. With the amount of bodies the industry has, the only good thing for investors is that they have not unionized. Capital is cheap and land in the form of computers is cheap. But they have labor coming out you-know-what and that's the most expensive piece of production these days.

STEVE: Any last jewels I have failed to extract that you would like to offer the financial sector investor?

DAVID: I cannot emphasize enough that the financial services industry is a mature business that will move slowly. If you have a short-term time horizon of a couple of quarters, then this is not your game and it should not be what you want to own. This industry has a proven history of making money and losing money. I think the time to buy is when the industry is under pressure. The nice thing about this industry is that we know how they make money, but the more important thing is that we know how they lose money. When we talk about Microsoft, I don't think people understand how Microsoft is going to lose money. What series of events must take place in order for them to have a bad quarter? You can't figure it out, so no one will be able to predict it. The same in reverse is true of Amazon.com. Nobody knows how they are going to make money. So it is hard to predict it. But if housing prices start to fall and the yield curve inverts, then I can tell you what will happen to the financial stocks. It is easy to understand. There isn't any mystery here. So the game is just to stay with it. And buy it big when it is under stress, and you may want to lighten up or just sit tight when things are good. Play that cycle over 10 or 20 years and you will do pretty well.

STEVE: You've been most kind. Thank you for your time and such good detail.

DAVID: You're welcome.

CHAPTER 6

Playing the Aging Population: Investing in Health Care

"Healthy, wealthy, and wise." Aspirations for mankind (and womankind) since the dawn of time. Nearly two and one-half centuries ago, the most famous American in the world, Benjamin Franklin, said that anyone following an "early to bed, early to rise" regimen could achieve these three worthy goals. It's not quite that simple, but notice that Franklin listed health first!

Wealth through Health (Stocks)

It's not our job here to urge you to exercise, keep your weight down, or eat more fruits and veggies. However, we are convinced that this book's wealth prescription must include a strong dose of stock ownership in health science companies. No other sector has such built-in demand for its product. And, except for technology, no other sector routinely sees such astonishing breakthroughs. Open-heart surgery is common; appendicitis patients are routinely out of the hospital in 24 hours. Our granddaughter (and niece) weighed 19 ounces at birth—born 16 weeks early—and now is a healthy 13 pounds just one year later. Three years ago, even the best doctors and nurses couldn't have saved her.

Coupling medical innovation with aging populations worldwide creates a near-perfect investment scenario. Health care innovators that do what technology companies routinely do year after year—provide better products that cost less—will certainly be big winners. Even costly innovations can be very profitable for health care companies. Given the life-or-death importance of health care, no other sector has the ability to earn big profits from expensive innovations. As long as the cures are truly effective, most people will gladly part with some of their wealth for a little more health.

In case you need further convincing, consider the demographic argument. The 76 million U.S. baby boomers—born from 1946 to 1964—are aging. In 1999 the average baby boomer celebrates (or bemoans) birthday number 43. The fastest-growing segment of the U.S. population, by far, is the 85-and-over age group. According to government statistics, the total spent on health care for U.S. citizens averaged $4,000 per person in 1997. Certainly health care deserves its spotlighted role as one of the investment world's three favorite sectors—right alongside technology and financial services.

Biotechnology

The primary bridge between the health and technology sectors is the biotech company. Even though the *Wall Street Journal* lists the biotech industry group under technology, we have chosen to include biotech as part of the health care sector. Most health care fund managers buy biotech stocks, and both leading mutual fund ranking services—Morningstar and Lipper—group health care and biotech mutual funds together. At the end of 1998, Lipper rated 52 health/biotech mutual funds while Morningstar tracked half as many, 26. The returns from biotech stocks are the most volatile and correlate least with other health care sectors.

The Health of Health Care

Given the health care sector's problems in 1993 when Hillary Clinton spearheaded a massive health regulation effort in order to implement a federalized health care insurance system, it's no surprise that the years since then, 1994 to 1998, have produced fine returns for health care mutual funds. Growth sectors such as health care tend to rebound well after a dismal year or two. According to Lipper, health care mutual funds' five-year average (1994–1998) is a sparkling 20.1%. Only technology (25.2%) and financials (23.4%) have done better.

Ed Owens, Vanguard Specialized Health Care fund manager, stated in the August 1997 *Louis Rukeyser's Mutual Funds* newsletter that he believes health care is the best sector of the economy to invest in long term, owing to its superior growth and low cyclicality, as well as very good predictability. Our expert interviewee, Pat Widner, former comanager of the Warburg-Pincus Health Sciences fund, points out that health care expenditures are the highest single after-tax personal expenditure by American households—18% of disposable income—yet health care stocks are only about 13% of the U.S. stock market. She postulates that this imbalance—health care sector expenditures that are considerably higher than the amount of money invested in health care stocks—make it likely that health care stocks will continue to do well. A more health-conscious and educated consumer, huge amounts of venture capital funding medical research, and all those aging baby boomers also are key reasons, she believes, that the health care sector offers such promise.

Certainly, given the aging population in the United States, Europe, and Japan, health care expenditures will continue to increase as a percentage of GDP (gross domestic product). The 1997 growth rate of 5% for U.S. health care expenditures was the lowest since the 1960s; however, even at a 5% growth rate, health care expenditures will double in 14 years.

Data for the U.S. pharmaceutical industry show that the average American between ages 35 and 44 spends $275 annually on drugs, while the average citizen between ages 45 and 54 spends 42% more—$390 a year.* (See Figure 6-1.) Managed-care companies' efforts to cut costs have actually increased spending on drugs in order to prevent costly surgeries. For example, it's estimated that blood thinner prescriptions have prevented 40,000 strokes yearly—saving $600 million annually in hospitalization costs.

The Danger of Regulation

While biotech and medical delivery stocks are quite volatile, overall, health care stocks, particularly health care's "blue chips," the large

*Investor's Business Daily, July 13, 1998, p. B1.

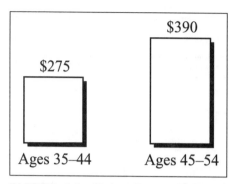

FIGURE 6-1 **Expenditures on Prescription Drugs**

pharmaceutical companies, are normally quite stable. The drug company stocks held up very well during the summer 1998 bear market. However, no sector faces higher risk from government regulation than health care. The public keeps demanding more and better health care while governments keep looking for ways to contain the health sector's budget-busting costs. In 1993, when it appeared that the Clinton administration's attempt to pass federally regulated national health care insurance might succeed, the stock prices of big pharmaceutical companies took a real beating. (See Table 6-1.)

Currently, there appears to be a national movement toward more open markets and away from regulation (utility deregulation and vouchers for charter schools are current classic examples). However, such is not the case with health care. It seems destined to become more regulated. One of the most popular campaign platforms during the 1998 election was the consistent support, by both Democrats and Republicans, for more regulation of HMOs to give their customers "more rights." It's no wonder that HMO stocks did poorly in 1998. But those very same HMO stocks were big winners in 1993 when it appeared that every American would be forced to join a HMO if the Clintons' health care legislative proposals passed. There is little doubt that ever-changing and expanding government regulation is one of the biggest dangers to the profits of health care companies and to the investors who own their stocks.

Investing Strategies

We believe that health care is certainly a must for every serious sector investor. The best choice for beginning investors is to buy a diversified

TABLE 6-1 The Threat of Regulation and the Performance of the Three Largest Pharmaceutical Companies

Company	1992 High	1993–94 Low	1998 Low	1998 Close
Merck	$56^5/8$	$28^5/8$	$101^3/8$	$147^1/2$
Glaxo Wellcome	$35^1/4$	$14^5/8$	$47^1/8$	$69^{15}/16$
Pfizer	$21^3/4$	$13^1/8$	$71^1/16$	$128^{15}/16$

no-load health care fund. Our favorite four are Invesco Health Sciences, Vanguard Specialized Health Care (now closed to new investors), Warburg-Pincus Health Sciences, and the new Janus Global Life Sciences (begun December 31, 1998). Or you might choose to buy a blue-chip pharmaceutical company. One of only two stocks that our administrative assistant owns is Merck. She paid $105 a share for it early in 1998; by December it was trading at $156 a share. That's a 49% gain. (Merck is available without going through a broker—you can buy it as a no-load DRIP by calling 800 774-4117.) We also own Abbott Labs and Pfizer, which have been consistent winners.

A more aggressive strategy is to buy a pure subsector mutual fund like Fidelity Select Biotechnology or Fidelity Select Medical Delivery (both have 3% loads) or a small-cap subsector no-load fund such as Firsthand Medical Specialists. Just like individual stocks, these funds are quite volatile.

Of course, the greatest risk of all is to buy a small, unproved health care stock—as we learned the hard way. In 1993, we bought warrants for Lidak Pharmaceutical for $1.50 a share, then bought some more at $3 and made a large purchase at $5.25. Unfortunately, Lidak's wonder drug to cure Herpes failed its FDA trials. The warrants became virtually worthless when the company redeemed them at 5 cents a share in 1994. At one time we had an $18,000 profit when Lidak's warrants reached their peak at $7.75 a share, but this was the stock that would make us rich. So we didn't sell and as a result suffered our single largest investment loss ever—just over $17,000. Never again will we be so stupid and so greedy!

Expert Interview

To find insight into to the world of health care, we turn to our only female expert, Patricia Widner. Her unique background in the health care field gives Widner even greater credibility to speak to the subject at hand.

SNAPSHOT

Patricia F. Widner was a managing director with Warburg-Pincus. She comanaged the Warburg-Pincus Health Sciences fund from 1996 to 1999. She joined Warburg-Pincus in 1991 as a senior health care analyst. Before that, she spent 16 years in the health care industry and on Wall Street. Pat was a registered dietitian at Peter Bent Brigham Hospital in Boston; a sales representative for Abbott Laboratories; a marketing director for Whittaker Health Services, a start-up HMO that was later sold to the Travelers Group; and a venture capitalist investing in health care companies for Citicorp. She has an MBA from the Wharton School, University of Pennsylvania, and a BS from Marymount College.

STEVE: Can you give us a brief history of the health care sector and how it's evolved over the past decade or so?

PAT: I think there are two important themes. One is that historically health care has been a not-for-profit sector, and over the last decade health care has become increasingly for profit. That's a very big change. The second theme is that health care is becoming a more and more publicly traded industry. In the past, the industry had been largely private. This transition means more opportunity for the investing public.

STEVE: So was part of the Hillary Clinton scare back in 1993 the thought that health care might be regulated back to a mostly not-for-profit industry?

PAT: That was one of the thinking postulates that came out of Hillary's effort. What I think was very important to the effort was the debate over "the first 100 days" where we, as a country, were invited to study the issues and then decide on a health care plan. Newspapers carried articles about the various issues surrounding health care. And I think the media did a fabulous job of weighing the pros against the cons of each aspect of each argument regardless of the consequences for the health care system in either the for-profit or not-for-profit sector. The Hillary Clinton era, if you will, really opened up the debate to the U.S. population as a whole and brought tough issues out in the open instead of keeping them in the academic centers and in political circles. This was a very good thing for the country, and I think we came out of it with a lot of recognition that there was more than one way to look at the health care system.

STEVE: So do you think that debate was good for health care stocks?

PAT: Actually, most health care stocks traded down during that debate. You have to separate the fundamentals of the debate from the stocks. I think the debate was good because we, as a country, need to have some coherent policy going forward to handle the baby boomer generation's need for health care as it ages. Financing health care in a piecemeal fashion can last for another decade but it may not be sufficient enough to handle the next 30 to 40 years. Hillary's plan was the first foray into this debate and, as such, may have overstated the case for national health care in order to expand discussion.

There was a group of stocks that did exceedingly well during those years, though. And those were the HMOs. I call them collectively the buyer group: any entity that buys health care, whether it's pharmaceutical products or health care in general. The HMOs do the buying on behalf of the payers, which are the employers, the government, or individual policyholders. And so this buyer group actually outperformed the market during this time period because they were considered the key drivers of the Hillary Clinton plan and therefore they would receive more volume. So even though HMO prices would be regulated, they would benefit from the increased volume. Thus, you can't make the across-the-board statement that all health care stocks do badly during a regulatory discussion, but you do have to pick your stocks very carefully.

STEVE: So is there a danger of this discussion occurring again and, as a result, a big section of the health care stocks going south?

PAT: Yes. In fact, I think you saw this in the summer of 1998. Some of the effects of the balanced-budget bill were being felt, and it made folks very scared in the provider sector of health care.

STEVE: Could you define provider sector?

PAT: The provider sector is defined as those entities which serve patients—for example, hospitals and nursing homes. Some of these providers had funding cut effective in July 1998, when the balanced-budget provisions kicked in. That's the risk across the whole health care industry.

STEVE: Are there other major dangers that you see on the horizon?

PAT: It's a bit of a mixed bag. Regulation is the big risk that institutional investors do not like. Again, I want to stress the point that regulation will not adversely affect health care stocks across the board. Its effects are only in certain segments of the industry.

STEVE: So money can still be made in other sectors of health care?

PAT: Right. That is why we always stress our balanced approach in running the fund. We always invest in four different sectors of health care. This keeps us adequately diversified, since one cannot predict what regulation may come next.

STEVE: What are those four different sectors of health care?

PAT: There are the "buyers," like HMOs, which we talked about earlier. There are the "providers," which is any entity that serves health care. There are the "suppliers," which are the manufacturers. And then there are the biotechs, or the "innovators" as I call them, which have totally different financial characteristics and which don't really move with any of the other stocks.

STEVE: What, then, are the compelling reasons to invest in health care stocks? What arguments would you make in favor of your sector?

PAT: I think the primary argument is the very strong demographic story. Everybody knows the aging, over-65 population demands more health care. But I would like to submit to you that there are two demographic stories. One is the over-65 population and one is the 45-to-65 age population. There are increasingly new technologies being discovered to handle some of the diseases that heretofore have not been highlighted. For example, in the 45-to-65 population, there are new baldness drugs. There are new impotence drugs. There are new drugs to handle unstable angina. And these kinds of conditions are where a lot of the R&D money is going. So this is a whole new population that can benefit from a lot of the innovation. This innovation is the second theme that I believe to be a strong reason for investing in the health sector. Innovation is exploding in health care simply because the baby boomers are reaching their peak years in terms of intellectual capacity and productivity. There are many physicians and scientists from the baby boomers who are in the research field. Their discoveries are just exploding, so there is a supply-side economics in health care to some extent.

STEVE: Meaning?

PAT: Meaning that the more technologies and the more cures for diseases like cancer that are found, the more people there will be to use them. If the supply is there, it will be utilized.

STEVE: That is a great point. In other sectors, oversupply is a bad thing, but with health, there is a built-in demand for the cures to our diseases.

PAT: Right. That's why my third theme is the leveraging of the efforts of the U.S. venture capitalists. We have seen record funding flow into venture capital over the last five years, and about 20% to 30% of that money goes into health care start-up companies. And financing health care innovation has its rewards. Unlike any other country in the world, America is a capitalistic health care society. We reward innovation by making people rich. Nowhere else in the world is there this built-in infrastructure for innovation. So not only do we have a demand for science and a supply of scientific breakthroughs, we also have rewards for those who actually deliver. This is a very exciting time in health care because we have an elderly population, which is becoming more demanding, and we have a baby boomer population, which is delivering supply. And then we have the venture capitalists who are interested in making a return. It is a wonderful cycle.

STEVE: Is the increased, consumer-oriented advertising that we are seeing by the drug companies part of this theme?

PAT: Yes. It is exactly playing right into it. We believe health care is becoming increasingly retail. As you empower the consumer, the companies that can meet consumer needs will do very, very well in the new paradigm in health care.

STEVE: So what is your basis for deciding which individual companies to invest in within the health care sector?

PAT: We have six criteria for picking companies. One, we look for a minimum $300 million market opportunity to sell into. That is $300 million of potential sales per product line. For example, if I were looking at a company and it had three product lines, I would like to have a $900 million market opportunity—$300 hundred for each product. The second criterion is a breadth of product. The company should have more than one product to bring to market.

STEVE: Not a one-drug wonder.

PAT: Correct. Third, we look for proprietary positions in their product lines. We like a defensible product. Whether it's through a patent or whether it's through a timing advantage, we try to make sure the product offering is truly unique and not just a commodity. Fourth, we look for a very strong management team, and that is not just financial management or operational management. It includes management that has done clinical trials before and has experience with the FDA. We want management who knows how to lobby at times for what they feel is needed in Congress. So there are many different management skills that we find absolutely critical. The fifth criterion is collaboration with other companies. We don't want companies to reinvent the wheel. If management is trying to sell into 6,000 hospitals in the United States, shouldn't they partner with someone like Johnson and Johnson or Abbott Labs, companies that have tremendous leverage in hospitals? Why should a company create a new sales force to call on 6,000 hospitals? Finally, we look for earnings growth and consistency.

STEVE: How about the drug giants like Merck and Pfizer? Can they maintain such high valuations and such high P/E ratios?

PAT: P/E ratios are derived from both internal and external factors. External factors include the inflation rate, long-term interest rates, and what the economy is doing. It is not my job to call those kinds of factors that would affect the P/E. I look at the internal factors that have to do with P/E ratios. And those are really two things. One is the absolute growth rate of earnings and the second is the consistency of earnings. Based on history, the drug companies have been wonderfully consistent and have superior growth rates to most sectors of the economy. And that is why their P/E ratios are very high.

STEVE: You pay for consistency.

PAT: Correct. The question then becomes: what is the growth rate for the S&P 500 going to be in the next 10 years? I can't predict it. But what I do believe is that the volume of pharmaceutical sales over the next 10 years will be greater than it is today because the U.S. population is aging. Thus one could argue that the growth rate of these companies will be superior to the economy as a whole and therefore, on a relative basis, pharmaceutical companies deserve a higher valuation. Health care outlays are growing faster than the economy as a whole. So wouldn't that argue that health care stocks should outperform the market based on the fundamentals alone over the next 10 years? And that is why everybody should have a position in health care.

STEVE: What percentage, then, of an individual's long-term portfolio should be invested in the health sector?

PAT: I have a couple of points that make the case for an overweighting in health care stocks. Right now, in December 1998, the S&P 500 has roughly a 13% weight in health care stocks. And most generalized portfolios only own a handful of those names. However, there are approximately 1,150 companies in health care in 1998, not including the foreign companies. Only 38 of those health care companies are represented in the S&P 500. But a lot of the innovation that is so crucial to the health care sector comes from smaller companies. And about 80 percent of these 1,150 companies in the United States are under $500 million in market capitalization. And to the extent that you want to participate in health care's innovation, you must invest in smaller market cap companies, which are the ones that are coming up with many of the new ideas. So that's one argument. You should be more diversified than you normally get in one generalized capital appreciation fund or growth and income fund. You are probably picking up some of the S&P's exposure to health care stocks in the broader fund, but you are not getting the whole number. I would argue that you should put some extra money in a health care sector fund in order to be fully leveraged in the sector.

STEVE: Would you say 20% of one's total portfolio?

PAT: That depends on one's risk tolerance. Every person's individual situation is unique.

STEVE: What if someone wants to be aggressive?

PAT: For the long-term investor, a possible target number is 18%. My basis for that number comes from the following statistic that I personally find fascinating. According to numbers from 1996, about 18% of a U.S. family's personal expenditures went toward health care in one form or another. It is the number 1 expenditure. Numbers 2, 3, and 4 are housing, food, and transportation. So Americans spend more of their after-tax dollars on health care than any other item. Now obviously, that is on average. Some people spend more and some less. So if you are spending 18 cents of every dollar that you take home on health care, and I am the investor in health care stocks, then I am making money off you—because I've got my money in the health care stocks that are making money on that 18% personal expenditure.

STEVE: So you say that since 18% of personal expenditures are going toward health care, then 18% of investments could logically go toward the health care sector.

PAT: Again, only for those who understand the risks. During times of regulatory debate, like what appears will be happening in the next year or so, a market-neutral weighting in the health care sector would be advisable. Still, for long-term investors, 18% would be a reasonable number. How you can get there is by deducting the weighting of health care in your capital appreciation and growth and income funds. You would have to check their prospectuses, but many growth funds probably have a 9% to 13% weighting in health stocks. You then deduct that percentage from the 18% target, and for the aggressive investor, that should leave some extra to invest in a health care sector fund. Obviously, we are talking broad generalizations here. Each individual should analyze their entire portfolio when determining exactly how much extra to put into the health care sector.

STEVE: Any other last words of advice or warning for the average investor?

PAT: Yes. What's most important to remember here is that health care is a long-term investment. It is not something that beats the market every year.

STEVE: But that is what we all want!

PAT: I know. The statistics show that from 1985 through 1997, health care stocks of similarly sized companies have on average outperformed their peers by about 60 percent. But it does not happen every year. The statistics show that the years where there is a big political issue and/or it is an election year, health care does not typically outperform the market. However, if you hold on, there is a probability of good performance for reasons we previously discussed. Also remember, timing the market is very difficult. In health care, you can't time the upside because there is no timing event that acts as a catalyst.

Finally, I want to stress that health care is a great industry. It is one of the largest industries in the United States. It is one of the fastest-growing industries in the United States. And everyone is paying into it. Therefore, one should exploit the increasing demand as well as the innovation explosion. The average investor should simply invest a little, then hold on because the ride is very, very exciting.

STEVE: And some of that holding on should be done in Warburg-Pincus Health Sciences.

PAT: Well, we would be very grateful if we had the opportunity to serve any of your readers.

STEVE: Thank you for your time and your insights. We appreciate it.

CHAPTER

7

Traveling the World: Investing Internationally

ike Columbus or Magellan, the international investor must have a certain curiosity about what is on the other side of the ocean, along with the will to travel there. International investing also requires a certain amount of courage akin to that of the great explorers. Foreign investing is after all—well, "foreign" to many of us. And it is that unknown that holds us back. But did Christopher Columbus even once regret facing his fear? We don't think so. There were unimaginable opportunities in 1492 and there are slightly more imaginable ones today—just across the sea. O.K., south of the border too. Regardless, let us hoist the anchor aboard, and sail!

Think Outside the U.S. Box

As we explained in Chapter 1, buying the stocks of companies headquartered outside the United States is not really a sector investment choice at all; instead, deciding to invest internationally is actually an asset allocation decision. Because about 50% of world stock value comes from foreign stocks, neophyte U.S. investors severely limit their options if they target only U.S. businesses. Most U.S. citizens routinely buy gasoline from BP (British Petroleum) or Shell (a Dutch company). Why should they ignore the profit potential in those stocks?

Unless they chose to sell their stock, Chrysler shareholders automatically became international investors in November 1998 when the Daimler-Benz and Chrysler merger was consummated. The new corporation, Daimler-Chrysler, is a German company (German tax laws are more favorable to corporations than U.S. laws) even though Chrysler will continue to have its headquarters in Detroit and compete vigorously against Daimler's Mercedes dealerships in the United States.

As the communication revolution continually shrinks our planet, the ongoing globalization of the world's premier businesses is bound to continue as mergers and takeovers blur the national identities of many corporate giants. Does it really matter to investors that Daimler-Chrysler chose Germany rather than the United States as its corporate locale? (London was the leading choice before it became apparent that the costs to relocate to England were prohibitive.)

The Currency Issue

Certainly our more astute readers will argue that a corporation's location does matter to investors because its overall profits are reported in the currency of its home country. If the German mark falls dramatically against the U.S. dollar, then Daimler-Chrysler's profits—converted from marks to U.S. dollars—would be lower. Of course, a stronger dollar would also mean that profits from Chrysler and Mercedes sales in the United States would convert to more German marks—boosting Daimler-Chrysler prof-

---

"Of the world's 35,639 regularly traded stocks, only 12,863 are based in the U.S., reckon the investment researchers at Wilshire Associates in Santa Monica, California. That means nearly two-thirds of all investment opportunities are based outside our borders. 'Do you really think,' asks Rick Spillane, who oversees international investing for the Fidelity funds, 'that there are no good companies out there?'"

Many beginning investors may not know the difference between global and international mutual funds. However, the distinction is significant. Most international funds buy only non-U.S. stocks; a small minority of international funds will buy a few U.S. stocks, almost always less than 10%. Global funds, on the other hand, typically hold 20% to 40% of their portfolios in U.S. stocks. According to Morningstar research, the average global fund held 35% of its portfolio in U.S. stocks at the end of 1998.

its in marks and thereby helping offset the impact of the weaker mark on U.S. owners of Daimler-Chrysler stock.

The New Euro

In reality, the example used in the previous paragraph is no longer completely valid. The value of the mark against the dollar was critical to U.S. investors in Daimler-Chrysler for a few weeks after the merger in November 1998. Beginning January 1, 1999, a new international currency—the euro—became the corporate currency for 11 European nations.

Daimler-Chrysler's profits are now calculated in euros—a so-called virtual currency from 1999 to 2001. Euros cannot be purchased over the counter from European banks until January 2002. Until then, the euro will operate only as a trading and banking currency—a common currency for stock and bond prices—and it will be the currency of choice for traveler's checks and credit cards in the 11 countries that have adopted it. Beginning in 2002, both the euro *and* each country's native currency—francs in France, marks in Germany, lire in Italy—will be used for everyday consumer transactions. However, beginning six months later, on July 1, 2002, the European monetary union countries' age-old currencies will no longer be accepted—totally replaced by the new euro. (See Table 7-1.)

The euro makes trade so much more efficient throughout continental Europe—imagine the higher costs of trade between Chicago and Los Angeles if Illinois and California used different money. There is now only one currency accepted virtually everywhere in the world—the U.S. dollar. However, if Great Britain adopts the new currency, then undoubtedly the euro will win widespread global acceptance.

TABLE 7-1   The New European Monetary Union

Current 11 euro countries	Austria, Belgium, Finland, France, Germany, Ireland, Italy, Luxembourg, Netherlands, Portugal, and Spain
Countries most likely to adopt the euro by 2005	Denmark, Great Britain, Greece, and Sweden
Value of the euro against the U.S. Dollar on January 4, 1999	$1.16675
Timetable	
January 1, 1999 to December 31, 2001	Noncash transactions only (i.e., charge card purchases and traveler's checks for consumers)
January 1, 2002 to June 30, 2002	Euro notes and coins coexist with home country's currency
July 1, 2002 and after	No home country currency accepted; only the euro is legal tender in the 11 countries listed above

Anticipation of the adoption of the euro has helped spark European stock markets. The average European open-end mutual fund returned a sparkling 20.1% four-year annual average from 1995 to 1998. However, for the first five years of the decade (1990–1994), the average annual return for European mutual funds was a miserable 2.7%.

Methodical Investing

Before beginning investors focus in on just one area of the world—Europe, for example—we recommend that they first choose a diversified no-load international mutual fund. Therefore, the choice of where to invest worldwide is delegated to full-time professionals who spend all their working hours studying international markets. The mutual fund manager and staff then buy foreign stocks wherever they find stocks that meet their criteria. One reason our chapter guru, Mark Yockey, did so well in 1998 is that he had more than 80% of his Artisan International portfolio positioned in European stocks. His fund was up 32% in 1998 and averaged 22.5% annually for three years (1996–1998). (See the end-of-chapter interview for why Yockey avoids buying Japanese stocks.)

After picking a diversified international mutual fund, the investor may wish to target an area. For example, we own two emerging-markets funds that may choose companies located in Asia (except Japan), Eastern Europe, Africa, and Latin America. After a spectacular 65.5% return in 1993, the average emerging-markets stock mutual fund has actually lost money over the past five years, declining 10% annually from 1994 to 1998. We also own a closed-end Latin American fund, and the closed-end Morgan-Stanley Africa fund is one of our favorites.

Want to be even more aggressive as an international investor? Maybe you already own diversified international and area overseas funds, or perhaps you simply believe that U.S. stocks have become overpriced after S&P 500 mutual funds racked up a 10-year return (1989–1998) of 18.6% annually. Then consider buying individual foreign stocks or mutual funds that specialize in one country. Most single-country funds are closed-end. (See Chapter 2 for an explanation of the differences between closed-end mutual funds and their more traditional cousins, open-end funds). At the end of 1998 we owned the single-country Australia, Austria, and Chile funds (closed-ends), the Capstone New Zealand Fund (open-end), Malaysian World Equity Benchmark Shares (WEBS) that trade on the American Stock Exchange, and a supermarket in Chile that trades on the NYSE as an American Depository Receipt (ADR).

Buying blue-chip foreign stocks that trade as ADRs on the New York Stock Exchange—Germany's Daimler-Chrysler, England's BP-Amoco, Japan's Sony, to name just three—is certainly the lowest-risk way to invest in individual non-U.S. companies. We suggest you buy at least eight, diversifying both by country/region and by industry. One easy, low-cost way to build a portfolio of individual foreign stocks is by taking advantage of direct purchase DRIPs (dividend reinvestment plans). Call 800 774-4117 for a list of more than 100 foreign stocks that may be purchased initially for $1,000 or less, with additional share purchases available for $100 or less.

Asset Allocation

How much of your portfolio should be invested internationally? We believe that there is a strong likelihood that international funds will outdistance U.S. funds during the first decade of the twenty-first century. Yet, even though half the world's stock market wealth is outside the United States, we rarely recommend, even for young and aggressive investors, putting more than one-third of a stock portfolio in investments overseas. Typically, an international asset allocation of 15% to 25% seems to be a logical choice.

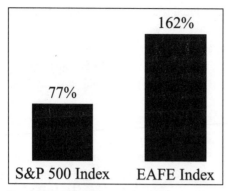

Data source: Standard & Poor's: MSCI.

FIGURE 7-1 **Domestic Versus Foreign Markets, 1970–1979**

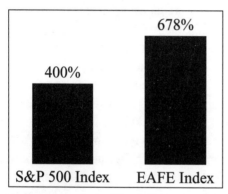

Data source: Standard and Poor's; MSCI

FIGURE 7-2 **Domestic Versus Foreign Markets, 1980–1989**

The 25-year correlation (1974–1998) between zigs and zags in U.S. and foreign stock markets is only about 45%; however, increasing globalization has raised that correlation to about 60% over the past five years (1994–1998). Diversification is important to all investors: "The fact is you won't lower your risks by keeping all your money in U.S. stocks, you will raise them."* Given the sensational U.S. market run from 1995 to 1998, and lousy results everywhere else, except for Western Europe, every serious investor should consider becoming an owner of some of the great businesses located outside U.S. borders. During the 1970s, U.S. markets as represented

*Money, December 8, 1998, p. 75.

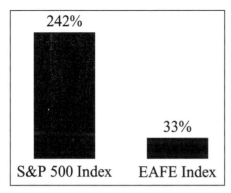

Data source: Standard and Poor's; MSCI

FIGURE 7-3   Domestic Versus Foreign Markets, 1990–1997

by the S&P 500 were up 77%, whereas foreign markets as represented by the EAFE index, which has a heavy Japanese weighting, were up 162%. In the 1980s, major foreign markets returned a whopping 678% while U.S. markets rose 400%. (See Figures 7-1 and 7-2.) That's 20 years of outperformance by the foreign markets. But the 1990s tell a different tale. Through the end of 1997 the S&P 500 was up a total of 242%, yet foreign markets struggled, gaining only 33%. (See Figure 7-3.) So is now the time for internationals to outperform again? Could we be due for another international spurt? Perhaps.

Expert Interview

Should the overdue international spurt materialize, Mark Yockey seems well positioned to take advantage of it. Many mutual fund aficionados regard Mark as one of the best talents in the international arena. We concur. The following interview should provide valuable insights for the serious international investor.

SNAPSHOT

Mark L. Yockey joined Artisan Partners in November 1995 and began managing the brand-new Artisan International fund on December 28, 1995. Previously, he spent nine years with Waddell & Reed, where he was a vice president and the portfolio manager of the United International Growth fund from 1990–1995. Mark also spent five years as a senior equity analyst for the State of Michigan Retirement System. A chartered financial analyst, he holds a BA in finance and an MBA in finance from Michigan State University.

STEVE: With all the international turmoil this past year, is now a good time to invest internationally?

MARK: People are obviously worried about what is going on in Japan and Southeast Asia and I don't want to minimize those things. But my first year of managing international money was 1990. That year we had a war with Iraq, a global recession, and accelerating inflation and higher interest rates. I would just like to compare what was going on then with what is going on now. There is no war going on. There's almost no inflation. The one thing that is similar to 1990 is that there is a concern about a possible recession. So far, the companies I have talked to are meeting their earnings expectations. And as long as companies' earnings continue to grow, stock prices will follow. So in times of turmoil, you have to look for opportunities to improve the quality of your investments.

STEVE: How is investing internationally different from investing in the United States?

MARK: International investing is much the same as investing in the United States. You look for companies that you understand. You don't buy businesses without knowing what they do. You look for companies that have a logic to their business and how they are managed. And you look for companies where there is an opportunity for growth. It's exactly like growth investing in the United States. International investing hasn't been sliced and diced as many ways as investing in the United States with small cap, large cap, midcap, and all the little iterations. We are an all-cap portfolio because we want to buy the best ideas regardless of their size. Another thing we look for is where the management has incentive to do exactly what we want them to accomplish. If they're successful, they make more money, and we like that because people tend to work harder if they think they are going to benefit from it.

STEVE: What other qualities in a company do you look for before investing?

MARK: The business itself is very important. That's why we like the financials. We like outsourcing. Both are growth sectors. With financials, there is a lot of growth potential, because the financial sector has been badly managed in Europe over the last 50 years. But now it's changing and becoming professionally managed, so there is a lot of growth opportunity there.

STEVE: How does risk compare between internationals and the United States?

MARK: I think risk has been less efficiently priced in international markets, because you're dealing with a lot of local investors who may be thinking about different issues than what U.S. investors are thinking about. And that might give us the opportunity to invest at a little better price than we might otherwise be able to get.

STEVE: From a historical perspective, is international investing becoming a safer bet? For example, is industry regulation helping?

MARK: Oh yeah, it's getting better. Especially with what's gone on in Asia. I mean the monetary meltdown in Asia should never have happened. Part of the reason it did was because there was very little transparency. Europe used to have very little transparency and now the level of information, the amount of information, and the detail has increased by a tremendous amount. Though in Japan, it's still very hard to get good information.

STEVE: Like Japan's accounting standards: is that what you're talking about?

MARK: They just don't tell you anything. They don't break down profitability by division. You could go through the whole list. You can read the whole annual report and you still don't know if they make any money or not. The degree and magnitude of disclosure is terrible.

STEVE: So the transparency issue is an additional risk for investing in Japan, whereas Europe has begun to address that problem.

MARK: Yes, absolutely. That is a very significant point.

STEVE: Japanese companies aren't very shareholder-friendly, then?

MARK: I don't think most companies in Japan even know they have shareholders! By contrast, European companies are becoming significantly more shareholder-friendly.

STEVE: Are there, then, compelling reasons to invest overseas versus hunkering down and simply investing in the United States?

MARK: Europe is particularly attractive on a secular basis because it is going through a process that we started 20 years ago in the United States. There is a whole secular trend evolving in Europe—toward being more responsive and more productive and more profitable. We think this process has only just begun in the last couple of years and we think it is going to go on for a long, long time. Returns on equity have gone up a lot in the United States and there is still a lot of room for improvement in Europe. You will find that sometimes assets overseas are mispriced and that presents good opportunities for investment.

STEVE: What about factors like the move to more private ownership of stock by the individual in Europe and the increasing number of 401(k)-type plans? Do these argue for investing internationally, or are they rather insignificant?

MARK: Actually they're very good reasons to invest internationally. Most of Europe has to set up private pension plans. A much smaller percentage of the European companies have private pension plans compared to their U.S. counterparts, because historically retirement has always been taken care of by the government on a pay-as-you-go basis. Also, the European population is getting older just like we are. So people are beginning to save for their own retirement, and that money is going to go into either stocks or bonds. And bonds at 5% aren't very attractive. If stocks can make 10% to 15% a year, then that's a lot more attractive investment. So there is a huge flow of money over the next 20 years that is going to go into investing in equities in Europe.

STEVE: How do you feel the EMU [European Monetary Union] will affect Europe's prospects?

MARK: It's only going to hasten growth. The EMU seems to be going ahead fairly smoothly, and most of the companies in Europe are on track to meet all of the requirements, even the French.

STEVE: How will the move to one currency impact investing in Europe?

MARK: Obviously, instead of having 11 currencies, there will only be one. I think if there is going to be a problem, it will be during this transition period [until 2002] when people will use this single currency and the other 11 currencies. Still, I don't foresee any real problems there. For our financial stocks, going to a single currency is an absolutely huge positive. It means that if you are a big bank in Spain, you will suddenly lose your size advantage because now you are part of Europe. You will only be a little bank in the economically united Europe. Everything is different. It means that if you are a big bank that is financially strong in Spain, you are going to try to acquire a bank in Italy or France or a bank in Germany. It also means that you must become more efficient when the single currency begins. So from a couple of different angles, it is hugely positive. The financial sector in Europe—and I will be diplomatic when I say this—has been under-managed for a number of years. And this is a big opportunity.

STEVE: Is the Y2K [Year 2000] problem a significant issue for European countries?

MARK: As far as we can tell, European companies, especially the financial companies, are allocating a tremendous number of resources toward dealing with the Y2K problem. And we have tried to benefit from all the money that is being allocated to resolving this question by investing in some of the companies that provide the labor and the technology to solve the problem. So there is a way to benefit from Y2K. If there is a place that worries me, it's Japan. I don't think the Japanese are doing enough to address the problem. They have actually cut back on their Y2K expenditures. I think there will be a huge panic in Japan as we get closer to 2000. Still, there is not anywhere in the world that you can go where people are not aware of it. So no one should be surprised when the year 2000 comes around. Overall, I'm cautiously optimistic about what is going on.

STEVE: In your fund, do you hedge the various currencies? And do you think that is important?

MARK: We don't hedge currencies. That has always been a source of contention with international investors—whether you should hedge currencies or whether you shouldn't. My own personal experience is that hedging is very expensive and figuring out which way currencies are going to go on a short-term basis is a very tough thing to do. It's a little like trying to predict which way the stock market is going to go tomorrow. I think there are probably currency traders in New York who are a lot better at it than I am. For me, the best way to spend my time is doing what I do best, which hopefully is picking good stocks.

STEVE: What about ADRs [American Depository Receipts]? Is that a good way for American investors to gain access to international equities?

MARK: Sure it is. Absolutely. Not all companies have ADRs, but more and more do because companies want to make it as easy as possible for U.S. investors to buy them. It doesn't matter to us whether we buy the underlying share or the ADR. It is totally immaterial. The only thing that is relevant is where will more liquidity be found and where will we get a better price. If we buy a large number of shares, sometimes an ADR is not very liquid and we are better off dealing in the local underlying share. Sometimes we pay a little lower commission if we buy the ADR. But other than that, it's the same decision.

STEVE: Since you don't hedge currencies anyway, it doesn't really matter to you.

MARK: No, it doesn't matter. You still own the foreign currency when you own the ADR. Of course, you could buy the ADR of Novartis, and then short the Swiss franc if you wanted. But for the average investor, I would not advise it. Just keep in mind that whether you own Nestlé in Switzerland or whether you own the ADRs of Nestlé, you own Swiss francs. So investors shouldn't think that because they own the ADRs, they don't have currency risks. If you own Nestlé, you own Swiss francs.

STEVE: What about selling a stock? What are your criteria for getting out of a company?

MARK: When companies stop doing what I think they should do. When they start violating some of the rules and start diversifying into some of the businesses they do not know. When they start making bad investments…

STEVE: So a lot of poor management decisions would cause you to dump the stock?

MARK: …A lot of poor management decisions, when they lose their focus, and also sometimes we make mistakes. Sometimes we think that a business looks very attractive and it isn't that attractive after all. And hopefully, sometimes we are successful and the stock price goes up a lot and it no longer represents good value for growth.

STEVE: Are there any other dangers unique to international investing of which our readers need to be aware?

MARK: International investing sounds mysterious, but it isn't. People should pay special attention *not* to follow the crowd. For a long time, emerging markets were the flavor of the month. You had to own them. Unfortunately, they became the flavor of the month after they had already gone up. It's good for people to take a step back and think about what they own. People shouldn't chase the last best thing that happened.

STEVE: With the increased impact of foreign economies on U.S. companies' profits, are we indeed becoming a global economy?

MARK: Yes, we are. And that's good. The United States has certain strengths. And capital is going to go where it gets the best return. In the United States, capital is going to high value-added areas. In Asian countries without much infrastructure, they tend to be good at things that are not high value-added. It's more labor-intensive. That's very positive, because labor is very cheap there. So this whole idea of specialization by doing what you do best is a good thing. People so often tend to focus on the negatives. But the fact that a lot of shoe factories closed in the United States over the last 20 years is a positive. Some people were laid off, but some people were retrained and are now writing software. And that is how countries grow. You go where you can add value and where your product is going to be valued. For Compaq to sell another PC and Microsoft to sell another software program adds more value than for us to make shoes in Missouri.

STEVE: What about returns going forward? What can be reasonably expected by the international investor?

MARK: It runs in cycles. In the 1980s, internationals did way better than the United States, and so far in the 1990s, it's gone back—that's a tough question. I always hate to give numbers. You see, the big thing that has held back the international markets the last 10 years has been Japan. Japan's economic condition has been getting worse since 1989. And it probably still has not hit bottom. When Japan hits bottom and they restructure, we will spend the time we need to find companies to invest in—when the Japanese companies change their behavior.

STEVE: In your opinion, what percentage of an investor's long-term portfolio should be invested overseas?

MARK: Well for me, I'm quite biased. So I have a considerable part of my assets invested internationally. But I think that 20% to 25% of a person's investments should be in an international fund.

STEVE: Any last words of advice or warning for the average investor?

MARK: People should not worry about which way the market is going, or the headlines. Invest in good companies. Don't read the headlines to make your investment decisions. Buy good companies. Invest in companies that have a strategy and good management.

STEVE: Or good mutual fund managers such as yourself?

MARK: I can't say that, but I wouldn't disagree with it.

STEVE: Thank you, Mark, for your time and the good job you are doing with Artisan International.

CHAPTER 8

Working as a Commercial Landlord: Investing in Real Estate

Imagine yourself sitting atop a vast empire of commercial property. You own a few high-rises in Chicago, a couple of golf resorts in Arizona, and some condominiums on the south Florida coast. You are a player. "Satisfied" is not a word found in your vocabulary. So you gamble on a billion-dollar hotel in the middle of New York City.

"Impossible," you say. "I could never afford to buy such high-priced property." Ah, but you are wrong. Thanks to the real estate investment trust (REIT), you can easily own a tiny piece of all these properties and more. You can become a commercial landlord.

REIT Defined

A REIT (pronounced "reet") is a company that manages and owns real estate properties. REITs pool the capital of many investors, offering participation in large and diversified real estate holdings that would not otherwise be available to the small investor. There are several different types of REITs, including apartment, factory outlet, health care, hotel, industrial, mortgage, office, and shopping center REITs. Publicly traded on the various stock exchanges just like other stocks, REITs give the small investor an opportunity to share in commercial real estate profits.

Taxation of REITs

In 1960, Congress passed a law approving the "conduit" or "pass-through" tax treatment for qualified real estate trusts. This means that as long as the REIT meets certain IRS requirements, the REIT itself is not taxed at the corporate level. Instead, the REIT's income "passes through" directly to the individual investor, who then is taxed at his or her individual tax rate. However, any undistributed income from the REIT is taxed at corporate tax rates. By not retaining their income, REITs avoid for their shareholders the double tax whammy whereby U.S. corporations pay almost a third of their profits in taxes before individual stock owners pay ordinary income taxes on the dividends. Side-stepping that double taxation is particularly important to REIT investors needing income; most REITs are now paying yields at least 1% better than CDs.

Risks

There are certain risks to investing in commercial real estate. Easy money and oversupply can tag-team to pin REIT profits to the mat. Cheap money becomes even cheaper as interest rates fall, leading to oversupply as commercial developers overbuild. Oversupply can then produce lower occupancy rates that dry up profits, leading to even lower REIT share prices.

Oversupply can appear quickly, especially if an unforeseen economic event wreaks havoc on the local or national economy. In this scenario, lack of demand is more to blame than is overbuilding. In the mid-1980s, Texas real estate went bust after oil prices fell sharply. Just a few years earlier, everything seemed rosy as oil profits skyrocketed. To service the expanding local economy with the needed commercial infrastructure, Texas developers raced to meet the oil-boon-induced demand. Commercial real estate went up so fast it was impossible to gaze upon any major Texas town without seeing several cranes dotting the skyline. Then, when falling oil prices caused a king-size Texas depression, no one was left to occupy all that space. The same could be said of southeast Asia in at the close of the 1990s. High-rises

Three other terms unique to the real estate sector are defined here:

A real estate operating company (REOC) is much like a REIT without the favored tax status. So whereas REITs must pay out 95% of their income as dividends, REOCs must pay taxes at the corporate level. But REOCs then have the freedom to reinvest their profits from year to year, allowing them more avenues for potential growth. REITs, on the other hand, generally pay higher dividends than REOCs.

Funds from operations (FFO) is a term used by REITs to define the cash flow from their operations. Most comparable to earnings for other stocks, it is calculated by adding depreciation and amortization expenses back to a REIT's stated earnings, as well as excluding gains or losses from property sales or debt restructuring.

Cash available for distribution (CAD) is basically FFO minus nonrecurring expenses and certain other rent adjustments.

sit almost empty as demand for new commercial property has all but vanished, leaving virtual ghost buildings. The boom turned to bust so quickly in the fall of 1997 that many projects ceased halfway through construction.

Size, or lack of it, can be another risk for a real estate investment trust. Mack-Cali Realty, Starwood Hotels, and Public Storage: these are three of the largest REITs available to the public. Yet the average person has never heard of these companies. Granted, REITs rarely have a nationally branded product, but REITs are also generally much smaller than well-known companies like Coca-Cola and Microsoft. In fact, according to Morningstar, the median market capitalization for all real estate mutual funds as of 1998 is a paltry $1.2 billion—right at Morningstar's cutoff for small companies. The relative smallness of real estate companies adds to the potential for disaster. Hazards such as poor management, lower occupancy rates, and unexpected economic conditions are magnified with smaller companies. So when considering a REIT investment, remember: the smaller the real estate company, the greater the risk.

Rewards

As harrowing as the risks may seem, there are certain potential benefits that may make REIT investing worth the risk. The main benefits number at least six:

1. An opportunity to participate in a professionally managed, diversified portfolio of real estate, and the ability to invest in large real estate operations.

2. Much higher current income than is available through other stock investments.

3. The potential for capital appreciation over time.

4. Liquidity and marketability—unusual traits in other types of real estate investment.

5. An opportunity to buy into an investment class that is by law composed of tangible, real assets and to buy in with relatively small amounts of money.

6. A stock investment that provides significant diversification compared with other U.S. stocks.

This last point is significant. Notice that of all the sectors in Table 8-1, real estate is the least correlated with the S&P 500. Its five-year correlation number is only .51. This lack of correlation has been a key selling point for investing in real estate. The argument goes that since real estate marches to its own drummer, it could very well be moving up when other stocks are moving down. Of course, the opposite could also occur.

Past Performance

As with most sectors, past performance for real estate has been varied. The average real estate mutual fund tracked by Morningstar was up 30.6% in 1996 and 21.9% in 1997. But 1998 tells a different tale. The average real estate fund plummeted 15.9%, underperforming the S&P 500 by 44.5%. Table 8-2 shows past performance for the average REIT mutual fund as tracked by Morningstar, as well as the Wilshire REIT index compared with the S&P 500 index. And since REITs are often thought of as a hybrid between stocks and bonds, the Lehman Brothers Mortgage Backed Bond index is included as well. Part of the reason for such poor recent performance has been oversupply and an expected slowdown in U.S. economic growth. In addition, more and more mutual fund companies created new real estate funds in the mid-1990s to keep and attract additional yield-hungry investors. From 1992 to 1998, the number of mutual funds specializing in real estate mushroomed from just 7 to 54.

TABLE 8-1   Five-Year Sector Correlation, December 1, 1993 to November 30, 1998

	Technology	Financial	Health Care	International	Real Estate	Utilities	Natural Resources	S&P 500
Technology	1.00	.63	.77	.59	.41	.46	.64	.76
Financial	.63	1.00	.73	.72	.60	.73	.63	.91
Health Care	.77	.73	1.00	.65	.60	.69	.70	.80
International	.59	.72	.65	1.00	.50	.55	.55	.73
Real Estate	.41	.60	.60	.50	1.00	.58	.61	.51
Utilities	.46	.73	.69	.55	.58	1.00	.50	.79
Natural Resources	.64	.63	.70	.55	.61	.50	1.00	.62
S&P 500	.76	.91	.80	.73	.51	.79	.62	1.00

Data source: Morningstar, Inc.

TABLE 8-2   Real Estate Sector Performance, December 31, 1998

	Real Estate Funds	Wilshire REIT Index	S&P 500 Index	LB Mortgage Bond Index
1 year	−15.90%	−14.22%	9.06%	8.63%
3-year average	11.17%	13.06%	22.60%	8.14%
5-year average	5.97%	7.71%	19.77%	7.26%
10-year average	8.82%	7.37%	17.11%	9.06%

Data source: Morningstar, Inc.

While not directly contributing to oversupply, these new funds have added to the availability of easy money for developers. The developers in turn have added to the oversupply that is so dangerous to relative REIT values.

Expert Interview

Andrew Davis bears a stellar pedigree. His grandfather, Shelby Cullom Davis, began running money in the mid-1940s, while his father began the top-rated New York Venture Fund in 1969. We can think of no one better equipped to explain the woeful state of real estate in 1998.

SNAPSHOT

Andrew A. Davis is president of Davis Selected Advisers, L.P. He is portfolio manager of the Davis Real Estate fund and the Davis Convertible Securities fund. He has more than 10 years of experience in investment management and has been employed by Davis Selected Advisers, L.P. since 1993. Previously, Andrew was a vice president at Paine Webber, Inc., managing both its convertible securities research and closed-end bond fund research departments. He is a graduate of Colby College in Waterville, ME.

STEVE: Can you give us a brief history or overview of real estate investing, especially in light of the limited corporate partnership fiasco of the 1980s?

ANDREW: The biggest difference is that the last time around those hired to manage the real estate did not own any shares in their particular limited partnership or real estate investment trust. Nowadays, it is completely different. The average insider ownership is 13% or 14%. That is a tremendous number when you think about senior management's incentive that results from owning stock in the company that they are managing. To me, that ownership eliminates a lot of conflict of interest, and conflict of interest is what ultimately undoes any partnership. The limited partnerships in the real estate arena were no exception. Conflict of interest is what killed them.

STEVE: Weren't these limited partnerships also like tar babies? I mean once you invested in them, you could not get out of them. Investing in real estate today is far more liquid.

ANDREW: That's an excellent point. Limited partnerships were very difficult to get out of, whereas today's real estate investment shares are literally traded every day on regulated stock exchanges. So you have a way of turning real estate from an illiquid investment owned by outsiders to a much more liquid, much more insider-owned investment vehicle. You put those two things together and everybody is pulling on the same rope and in the same direction.

STEVE: Continuing with our history lesson, how have returns from investing in REITs compared with the broader U.S. market over the past decade or so?

ANDREW: Except for this year [1998], real estate returns have been in line with the S&P 500 over the last 10 years. And if you think about it, that includes one whopper of a bear market in real estate. I would call it a depression. Still, I think that the difficulty with that past measurements is that, today, we are looking at an entirely new REIT world. In other words, if you go back a decade, we are talking about 1988. That was a different era in real estate. The class of real estate investment trusts that we are talking about now essentially started in 1992. That is when the real estate investment trust started to reemerge. The class of 1992, and a slew of others in 1993 and 1994, re-created the REIT. And again, that class re-created REITs in order to try to prevent what happened last time, which is when we had all the problems that we just talked about a minute ago: the conflict of interest that was rampant and the insider ownership that was nonexistent. I cannot emphasize strongly enough how important both of those characteristics are in the new breed of real estate investment trusts.

STEVE: What's happening in 1998? Why the underperformance by the REITs?

ANDREW: Well, I think the deal is this. Real estate is by nature an incredibly boring and dull business. In effect, the business is all about managing costs and collecting rents. And that, in and of itself, is not a 30% growth rate kind of vehicle. It's an 8% to 10% vehicle with a 5% dividend yield. Those are the kinds of returns that we are talking about. Now the thing is that everybody got very gung-ho about real estate coming off the bottom. We were in a major recovery mode. If you remember, real estate was in the doghouse for four years. I mean it really went into a depression that created all kinds of problems nationwide. The fact is that the real estate recovery is now over. And I think that is taking some time for people to understand. There were even momentum players in real estate. But that is over. And I don't think we are going to see the momentum guys again unless we have some kind of major league correction in real estate that would attract them. Still, when you have a slow-growth vehicle with a nice dividend yield, it is only natural to have a turnover of the type of investor that wants to own it. So no longer do we see growth managers playing there. What we see now is the traditional real estate buyer—one who has an income need, but wants a slight potential for growth in a less volatile product. I think that is what real estate today is offering, particularly now that valuations are so much lower than they have been in the last three or four years.

STEVE: So you see real estate as providing income at 5% or more, as well as providing the potential for appreciation.

ANDREW: That's right. We have got to stop thinking about real estate as real estate. We have to start thinking about it as an operating company whose product is real estate. You want to find great people to manage that company. You want cost cutters. You want people who know how to acquire property if that's what's attractive, or to develop property if that's what's attractive, or to merge with other companies if that's what attractive. You want great management in place.

STEVE: So when do you sell? Do you sell when a management team leaves, or when you become disappointed in the decisions that they're making?

ANDREW: There are a number of reasons we would sell. One would be if we had bought a company because it was an industrial play in Boston. In other words, we wanted exposure to the industrial market in Boston and this company was a way of doing that. Now if this company suddenly decides to become an apartment player in Atlanta as well, then that might be a reason for us to get rid of it, because that is not the kind of company we want to own. Second, and probably more important, is valuation. These companies are real estate companies. If they sell at 30 times earnings and they're growing at 10% a year, something is wrong. That is obviously an exaggeration, but we have seen examples of companies being bid up on momentum to fairly ludicrous levels. We just cannot own those no matter how much we would want to. We may love the company. We may love the strategy. We may love all these things. But my father said it very, very well: "You can own a great company at a lousy price and it is a terrible investment." That's not what we are in the business to do. We want to buy a great company at a great price. And that is hard to do. So we tend to find great companies on pullbacks. Then we buy them.

STEVE: What about the future for real estate? Are there any big changes on the horizon in the way business will be done?

ANDREW: I don't think so. There has been a lot of press lately about the paired-share structure being taken away from Starwood Lodging, Patriot American, First Union, and Meditrust. But that only really affects those four companies. I don't really see anything on the horizon that would make REITs less attractive. What I do see, maybe, are things on the horizon that would make REITs more attractive. For example, in order to become a REIT, all you have to do is jump through various hoops that the IRS puts out there for you. And if you jump through all of them properly, you don't have to pay any federal taxes. That is what being a REIT is all about. It's as simple as that. Now one of the hoops that you have to jump through is paying out about 95% of your net income. This is very difficult for any company, because you cannot retain any capital. And I would make an argument that your retained capital is your cheapest source of capital, because you do not have to go out and raise it and pay an investment banking fee. You do not have to spend enormous amounts of time away from managing the business, explaining to dopes like me why you are such a good company.

STEVE: You stated earlier that you were looking for a 5% yield and an 8% to 10% growth rate. So that means we could look for about a 13% total return over the next 5 to 10 years.

ANDREW: I would say that's right. We have been paying our investors 10% to 15%. That is about $5^{1}/2\%$ from yield and the rest from earnings growth. During the first quarter of 1998, FFO on average for real estate companies was up 18%. That is more than the S&P 500, mind you—much more. And real estate stocks were down. Down! Again, part of the market's beauty is that it is looking into the future and not into the past. But my point is that if I own every single share of every single real estate company out there—100% of all the companies—then I'm 18% richer during that quarter.

STEVE: Not too shabby.

ANDREW: Not too shabby is right! Now the irony in my mind is that the same people who tell me that REITs are overvalued are the people who are out there buying Yahoo! They don't seem to have any problem paying 25 to 30 times earnings for S&P companies on average, but when they look at a real estate company trading at $10^{1}/_{2}$ times next year's numbers, they get in a tizzy. So there is a real irony going on between investing in the S&P and investing in real estate. I don't know when that is going to clear up. But I would imagine that real estate companies will not recover until we get some of the growth and income players and some of the value players back involved in the game. People who are buying real estate generally are already in the game. In other words, I'm not going to move the real estate market even though all I invest in is real estate. What we need are other believers.

STEVE: So you do not invest in real estate related stocks like homebuilder Home Depot and others?

ANDREW: I could, but I haven't right now.

STEVE: You're only in REITs?

ANDREW: I'm in REITs and real estate companies. Remember, you don't have to be a REIT to be a real estate company. Being a REIT just means that you choose to jump through those IRS hoops to avoid paying taxes.

STEVE: What percentage or what role should investing in real estate play in the average investor's overall portfolio?

ANDREW: I think that real estate should make up anywhere from 5% to 15% of anybody's portfolio. It is exactly what we do in the Davis household. What I mean by the Davis household is our family. Our firm, which has about $20 billion in assets under management, has about a $1.5 billion of insider holdings in the same shares that you can buy. And real estate is a big chunk of that. When we sit around the breakfast table discussing asset allocation, we generally come to the conclusion that real estate should make up 5% to 15%. It should never be 30% and it should never be zero. We put it there for several reasons. One, real estate tends to be a diversifying asset class. It is less volatile. It does not move with the market. And it does not move with interest rates. And if anyone wants to debate me on that, 1998 was a perfect example. We've got interest rates going down—that should be bullish. We've got the stock market going up—that should be bullish. And what are REITs doing? Nothing. Not a thing. They stink. But I'm thrilled in a sense, because this year should prove to people that this is not about being countercyclical to interest rates. These things really do march to their own drummer.

STEVE: The correlation numbers I've looked at recently have really been low.

ANDREW: Yes. They are .2 or .3 [only 20% to 30% correlated with the S&P 500]. Our fund is a little lower. A quantitative MBA jockey would argue that you need to own this sector because it enhances return without increasing risk. That it is, if you believe in the capital asset pricing model. From a qualitative stance, we are talking about 13% annual returns. I know people are very used to 25% a year, but that ain't going to happen forever. The point is that it kills me because people chastise me for returning only 13%. We are talking 13% with 5% coming from the yield. I think any investor should own a piece of commercial real estate.

STEVE: We have gotten spoiled.

ANDREW: The only thing that is happening right now in stocks is the S&P 500. With the S&P, we've got the P [price] already in P/E, but we don't have the E [earnings] and we had better get it. In real estate, it is kind of the opposite. We've got the E, but we do not have the P. We can't seem to get any P out of this.

STEVE: But eventually…

ANDREW: That's right. And that is why in our growth fund we are buying real estate. In our growth and income fund, we are adding to our real estate position. And obviously, in our real estate and convertible funds we are too. I know I come across as somewhat bullish. But I am almost without words on what's going on here. I mean I understand the concept, but if you look at a 13% return for five years, then these stocks are worth more than what they are trading at right now. And I think once we get our split in valuations between the cans and the can'ts, then we are really going to shine.

STEVE: That brings me to my next question. There are obviously dangers looming on the horizon for the real estate investor, like recession. What are the primary dangers?

ANDREW: The biggest danger in real estate is supply. And the biggest creator of supply is easy money. There is no question that we have more supply now than we did two or three years ago. But I will tell you this. New supply in certain instances is very important. Now you are in North Carolina. I would challenge you to try to book a hotel reservation in New York City for next week some time. I will bet you that you cannot find one. That means that the development of new hotels in New York is probably a good thing. We could use them. When I go home to New York, I stay with my mother. It isn't because I can't afford a hotel room. It's because I can't get one. There just isn't any vacancy. So then development in and of itself is not necessarily a bad thing. Overdevelopment is a bad thing. And we are coming off several years, from 1989 to 1995, where there wasn't any development anywhere nationwide even though we had a pretty damned good economy. At some point, you have to start putting up new office buildings. Our business is a wonderful example. We've grown from 18 people five years ago to more than 200 today. We need a new building. Rather than inhabiting three buildings in different parts of Santa Fe, it would be nice to have one building. So that's an example of where development is a good thing. Now I would be stupid to tell you that we love development and the more the better. That is not what I'm saying. What I am saying is that a lot of people are overreacting to the amount of development that is going on right now. A lot of that development is build-to-suit development. In other words, tenants are already in place and are asking the developers to build a building for them so that they can take it over.

STEVE: But if the economy dries up, doesn't that...

ANDREW: Absolutely. If we go into a serious recession, then real estate will outperform. But it will still lose money. The one thing about development, though, is that it stops on a dime. What we do when we see a slowdown on the horizon is to focus on companies that develop products that are easy to stop. A 50-story office building, once it is in the works, is impossible to stop. It takes four or five years to get it built. With industrial space, on the other hand, it takes four months to build a building. You could stop that development pretty quickly. So we would shift our portfolio around to take advantage of that piece of information.

STEVE: With all this complexity, what do you think the best way is for the individual investor to take advantage of this important sector?

ANDREW: What I would suggest is that trading in a liquid form of real estate, other than a home, is probably the best thing for the individual investor to do. It's a very good business. There are a lot of good professional managers out there who do tremendous work. There are a lot of very, very good companies out there and you can own them. You can go to the New York Stock Exchange and buy them individually or you can buy them through mutual funds. Of course with a mutual fund, you get a manager who studies real estate day in and day out. What I would suggest is avoiding getting your money wrapped up in a limited partnership.

Also, let's say you own an office building or two. The fact is that the expense load that you have on that office building as an owner of two office buildings is going to be dramatically higher per dollar of revenue than for somebody who owns 150 of them nationwide. They can buy insurance nationally. They can buy toilet paper and light bulbs nationally. They can hire a national janitorial service. They can get great deals. It's sort of the WalMart concept of buying in huge bulk and then allocating supplies over many buildings. With one or two buildings, you aren't going to see those savings and that means you will be at a cost disadvantage in real estate. And being at a cost disadvantage in real estate is not a good position.

STEVE: That's it. Thank you very much for your time. It's been very informative.

ANDREW: Take care.

CHAPTER
9

Lighting Up Your Portfolio: Investing in Utilities

So you feel blessed. You've been fully invested in the hot U.S. stock market for several years and even plunked down big bucks to buy one of NASDAQ's big four—Dell, Cisco Systems, Microsoft, or Intel. Better yet, your $2,000 bet on one of those ultra high-risk Internet stocks made you 700% in 16 months. You were even lucky enough to sell near the top! Now you want to stash some cash. You are looking for an investment that has lower risk than the overall U.S. stock market but can still give you double-digit returns.

How about good ole American utilities? You know, the old-fashioned kinds that provide electricity, natural gas, and water. Don't laugh—give us a chance to make our case. Read the fascinating end-of-chapter interview with the two managers of the Strong American Utilities Fund before "just saying no." (Yes, we do understand that the only stock your grandparents ever owned was their local electric company.) Utilities are no longer "widows' and orphans'" stocks with very little risk and often mediocre returns. It's a totally new era for utilities: AT&T and the Baby Bells have recast themselves as technology companies while your everyday electric company is focusing on mergers and buyouts as it prepares for tough competition in the first decade of the twenty-first century.

Deregulation

There's a whole new world of deregulation heading our way! Just as we now have a choice among Sprint, MCI World Com, AT&T, and a host of smaller companies for our long-distance calls, most of us will soon have the same options as Californians now have for their electricity supply. We will be able to buy the electricity for our home from several different companies. There will be big winners and big losers in the new competitive free-for-all.

Most of you remember the 1970s, when airline ticket prices were totally regulated by the U.S. government. Back then, airlines had to petition the U.S. government even to lower fares! Price regulation is still true for most utilities in almost all states. However, we predict that having rates for electric utility generation set by the state will seem as antiquated an idea two decades from now as federally set airline fares seem to us today.

The Effects of Competition

Competition will largely end the political game that exists in most states. It's a game in which power companies are forced to play under profitability caps. Historically, the utility commissions in most states have set a predetermined profit level—often 11% to 13% after taxes. If less-efficient utility A wasn't making enough profit, then it would often be permitted rate increases; if well-managed utility B was making too much profit, then the state commission may have ordered a rate decrease. So the dilemma is fairly simple: (1) Where's the incentive for efficient B to get even better if there are no rewards for improvement? or (2) How is A punished for its inefficiency if it is permitted to raise its rates?

Until recently, utility generation was considered a natural monopoly. Certainly, this is no longer true. Technological breakthroughs have reduced capital requirements, and coordinating multiple ownership has facilitated ease of entry. The goal of deregulation is to provide better service at lower prices by giving the well-managed utility companies opportunities to expand their services and their market shares within their states and to compete successfully out of state. The merger wave has just begun. As competition heats up, the stronger companies will buy out their

> The ultimate engine that drives improvements in our standard of living is innovation, spurred by competitive production of our goods and services. No wonder communism was (and is) such an economic failure: imagine a system where the government sets prices for all goods and services and also controls their production and distribution. No better example of the contrast exists today than in South and North Korea. At the end of World War II both Koreas were about equal in per capita wealth. Today, thanks to its free market system and despite its recent depression, South Korea is more than 10 times richer than its northern neighbor. Recent reports indicate that thousands of North Korean children and the elderly die each month from malnutrition.

weaker counterparts, and mergers of equals will occur to reduce costs. Therefore, the utility sector is becoming more volatile while, at the same time, offering the potential for marketlike returns.

Adding to this volatility is the potential for lowered dividends. Typically, utility stocks were (and still are) purchased by older investors primarily because they need dividend payouts for income. Also, as we have done since 1984 by purchasing Duke Energy shares, investors often purchased their hometown utility stock, convinced it would provide steady returns with minimal risk. As utilities compete, they are likely to become more growth-oriented, paying out dividends that grow at a much slower pace than earnings. However, lowering dividends is a step that most utilities try to avoid, because it often leads to a steep stock price decline as many yield-hungry older investors sell their shares. In a few cases (e.g., FPL, a Florida utility), lowering the dividend has been justified as a method of increasing growth prospects. However, a dividend reduction usually indicates underlying difficulties. Even with the increased volatility that accompanies potentially lower dividend growth and intensified competition, electric, gas, and water companies' risk parameters are still not as high as those of most other stocks, given the absolute guaranteed demand for their services.

Interest Rates

Historically, movements in utility stock prices have shared with bonds an inverse relationship to interest rates. As interest rates fall, utility stock prices usually rise; and as interest rates move higher, utility share prices often decline. For example, in 1994, when the Fed raised interest rates six times, the 65 open-end utility mutual funds covered by Morningstar fell an average of 8.3%.

One reason utilities have been so interest rate sensitive has been their capital-intensive nature. They were forced to borrow heavily to finance costly generating facilities and related infrastructure. Nuclear energy plants were very expensive to build. However, construction of nuclear plants has been halted since the 1980s, as cheaper, and often smaller, alternatives have proved reliable. This trend toward cheaper construction costs, coupled with an increasingly efficient use of existing generating facilities as more and more utilities exchange power or merge, will work to reduce the capital-intensive nature of the business.

So as deregulation continues, we expect utilities to be less sensitive to interest rates but, at the same time, to become ever more correlated with the stock market's fluctuations. However, it will probably be a slow transition; for example, during the 19% decline in the S&P 500 from July 20 to August 31, 1998, utilities were easily the top-performing sector— helped by a dramatic fall in interest rates. And in the near term interest rates seem likely to stay low, a definite advantage for utilities during their transition to a competitive deregulated environment.

The Face of Change

Bill Reaves and Mark Luftig, comanagers of the Strong American Utilities fund, whom we interview below, argue that there will be restructuring in three areas: (1) electric generation, (2) billing, and (3) metering. Of course, the traditional utility does it all, but as deregulation takes place these three functions can be divided into separate businesses. The two service functions—billing and metering—are ideal candidates for competitive bidding by newer, more innovative companies. Undoubtedly, the government will continue to regulate the critical delivery side of the busi-

> **It can be argued that two events in 1979 doomed nuclear energy construction: the Three-Mile Island reactor accident in Harrisburg, PA and the release of the anti-nuclear-power hit movie, *The China Syndrome*, starring Jack Lemmon and Jane Fonda.**

ness by controlling the rates charged by the owners of the transmission lines that transport electricity to residences and businesses.

While the traditional power plants will continue as the primary source for generating our electricity, ownership and operation of these plants will increasingly be up for grabs. "Middlemen" companies will emerge to buy and sell power from suppliers. Their customers will be either end users or other wholesalers. As a result of all these changes, Reaves believes that some utilities will earn surprisingly high profits during the next decade but that utility investors will have a much tougher time identifying these "winners."

The British Are Coming!
The British Are Coming!

Another big change comes from foreign soil. Thanks to Margaret Thatcher's privatization initiatives in the 1980s, British electric utilities have far more experience with deregulation than their U.S. counterparts. They have learned to embrace competition and use it advantageously. Convinced that they can apply the lessons learned at home to compete successfully in the rapidly developing U.S. deregulatory environment, two of them, Scottish Power and National Grid Group (located in Coventry, England) announced billion-dollar U.S. takeovers in December 1998. They went bicoastal: Scottish Power announced a $7.9 billion buyout of PacifiCorp and National Grid is paying $3.2 billion for New England Electric. But American utilities are fighting back: Duke Energy, the largest U.S. utility, has bought power companies in both Australia and Chile.

Expert Interview

William (Bill) Reaves and Mark Luftig have 85 years of combined investment experience. Together, they manage the highly rated and solidly successful Strong American Utilities fund. There are not two better-suited people to guide us through the new deregulatory maze of the utility sector.

SNAPSHOT

William H. Reaves, senior comanager of Strong American Utilities fund, has been the president and chief investment officer, portfolio manager,

and utilities analyst of the subadviser W. H. Reaves and Co., Inc. (Reaves) since 1961. He has worked as a utilities analyst since 1946.

Mark D. Luftig, a comanager of the fund, is an executive vice president and utilities analyst at Reaves. Prior to joining Reaves in January 1995, he was the executive vice president and director of equity research at Kemper Securities, Inc.

STEVE: Mr. Reaves, you are the senior member of all our interviewees for this book. You have been running money since what—1928?

BILL: Oh, no. I'm not quite that old. I was just a child then. We've been running outside money for pension funds for 21 years. And we were obviously running money on an informal basis before that and I've been analyzing utilities for more than 50 years. We've been around the track.

MARK: The firm was founded in 1961.

STEVE: That brings me to my first question. There have been a lot of changes in the utilities industry since 1961. What do you currently include under the definition of a utility?

MARK: We include electric, gas, telephone, and water. We also include in our fund some energy stocks, and that makes us a little bit different than most. These energy stocks are the common stocks of big companies that pay out growing dividends.

STEVE: What do you say to those people who now consider telephone companies to be more technology companies than utilities?

BILL: We don't buy those. We buy the telephone companies that act more like utilities.

MARK: In other words, we don't own the telephone suppliers. We buy the local telephone companies and sometimes the long-distance companies.

STEVE: The old adage used to be that utility stocks were for widows and orphans. But that is not the case anymore. How have you seen things change in the utilities industry, especially in the light of deregulation?

MARK: One change is that utility stocks are more volatile than they have been in the past. But compared with a broad group of industrial stocks, they are still a lot less risky than the market as a whole. For example, the five-year beta on our portfolio is only 0.6. Also, the yield is several times that of the S&P 500. The electrics in the S&P are yielding 4% to 4.5%, whereas the S&P 500 as a whole is yielding about 1.5%. Another change is that utilities are less interest rate sensitive on a short-term basis than they were, and more utility companies are showing higher growth prospects than they have in the past. Today, some of the select companies that we are invested in are growing earnings at 8% to 10% a year. And some of the telephones are growing at 12% to 15%. That kind of growth was totally unheard of over the past 30 years.

STEVE: So how have returns compared with the broader U.S. market? Are they starting to close the gap?

BILL: Mark is going to give you our record, which will be something like the S&P 500.

MARK: Since 1994, utilities have underperformed the S&P. Over the past 10 years, our ERISA portfolios [retirement plans] have an average return of 16% a year. For 20 years, it is 18.6%. Our 10-year 16% compares to 18% for the S&P 500. And our 18.6% for the last two decades beats the S&P's 16.6% annual average. So...

STEVE: ...So not too shabby.

MARK: ...Not too shabby at all. Only five times in the last 20 years have we had less than a 12% return. In 20 years, we have had two losing years; our largest loss was 2.8%. Add to this that utilities are still doing what they are supposed to do, which is being defensive. Some people even use them as substitutes for bonds. For example, over the past 20 years, our 18.6% compares to 10.3% for the Solomon high-grade bond index. I think that you have to look at utility stocks as somewhere in between industrial stocks and long-term bonds.

STEVE: Now let's talk about the future. How do you see deregulation playing out, especially among the electric utilities?

BILL: Obviously, deregulation changes are here to stay. That is the way it is. The changes are pretty powerful and you can be sure that they aren't going to be stopped. Some states will be a lot later than others. Some states will be earlier. But it is coming. The consolidation of the industry is also a trend that cannot be stopped. In addition, the development of what we would call "services behind the meter" is very much on the way.

MARK: Let me just back up a little bit and go through it. There are three basic parts to the business. There is the generation portion, which produces electricity. There is the transmission portion, which uses the wires to carry it over long distances and frequently between utilities. And finally, there is the distribution portion, which is mostly the wires that go from the pole in your neighborhood to your house. Up until recently, virtually every utility was fully integrated. They all had distribution and transmission and virtually all of them had generation. Essentially, there was a natural monopoly in all parts of the business. Excess capacity developed, and at the same time, the cost of building generating stations declined. Now, utilities are able to build combined cycle plants in smaller sizes. These are gas-fired plants as opposed to big nuclear plants or 1,000-megawatt coal plants. That provided an ease of entry into the generation business. As a result, generation is no longer a natural monopoly. Potential competitors say: "We should be able to compete for that." It is a legitimate argument and that is what you are beginning to see—competition in the generation portion of the business.

STEVE: For example, our local North Carolina utility, Duke Energy, is selling electricity in California.

MARK: Right. The problem is that the markets are not wholly open yet. The reason for it is that you also have another dichotomy. And that is the difference between wholesale and retail. When a utility sells power to another utility or to another entity that's going to resell it, that's the wholesale side. Retail is a utility selling to someone who is going to use it. That could be someone in an apartment house or a factory. It doesn't matter. The wholesale portion is regulated by the Federal Energy Regulatory Commission (FERC) in Washington. It has mandated open access. This means that if you have three utilities A, B, and C, and utility A wants to sell power to utility C, then utility B must carry it over its lines. This has been accomplished. The current issue is retail and the state commissions regulate retail. In areas such as Pennsylvania and New York—California was the first place—the state regulators are coming along and saying: "We want retail competition." This means that the individual consumer will be able to choose a power supplier. And that has happened, thus far, only in a few states.

STEVE: So eventually it will be just like choosing AT&T or Sprint or whoever for long-distance services.

MARK: Correct. Except that in some states, the local utility will not to be allowed as a choice. Some states are requiring or providing incentives for local utilities to sell their generation. That is what is happening now in California.

BILL: ...And in Massachusetts.

STEVE: These utilities are being required to sell their generation to whom?

MARK: …To whoever wants to buy it. And it has all been done so far in an auction process. In Massachusetts, the utilities have already sold most of their generating plants to other companies. What has been happening is that the states with the highest utility charges have been pressured to move toward competition first because the perception is that this lowers rates.

STEVE: So is it wise to aggressively invest in these utilities right now? Or is this a dangerous game?

MARK: We think there are lots and lots of opportunities here. When this part of the business is deregulated, rates will no longer be based solely on rate of return. In other words, under the old system, a utility's rates were fixed by how much was invested in its plant. The state commission adjudicated a rate of return and then it determined the rates. The utility may or may not have earned the rate of return, but that is the way rates were set. If the utility became more efficient and its returns grew, its rates were cut. Essentially, since 1984, rates have been and are still being reduced. For the industry as a whole, rates have been coming down for the last 14 years.

STEVE: And that hurts profits.

MARK: It puts a lid on profits. On the other hand, with competition and market-based rates, the innovative companies will benefit from the higher returns they are going to earn.

BILL: …In the areas that are not regulated.

MARK: And that, of course, is because they are going to be competing only on price. Theoretically, everyone could come out all right. More efficient companies could earn higher profits, even by charging lower prices. All because there is a bigger incentive to be efficient. As part of this drive for efficiency, the industry has laid off a large number of people in the last few years. Under the old system, if a utility became more inefficient, rates were increased.

STEVE: I can see that as a problem for the consumer.

MARK: What often happened is that you ended up with the less efficient utilities charging higher rates and more efficient utilities charging lower rates with both earning essentially the same returns. Now, there is going to be a bigger disparity between what the various utilities earn.

STEVE: Then how do you evaluate which ones to buy?

BILL: You have got to know what you are doing.

MARK: The first thing that is much more important than it has been before is management. Management is going to make a very big difference. We also look at the costs of production. We visit each company before we invest and then stay in close contact. And we model expected earnings. Another important factor is potential earnings outside of the traditional regulated business. Some of the utilities have entered unregulated businesses in order to make money on a global basis. These would include companies like Duke, Southern Company, and Enron. They are also combining electric and gas....Getting back to our restructuring. There are new entrants into the unregulated generation business. AES is an example. In order for the whole system to work, the companies require equal access to the transmission system, which is a natural monopoly. It is very, very difficult to build major transmission lines today.

BILL: It is the "not in my backyard" thinking that prevents it.

MARK: People don't want utility lines crossing near their property. What is going to be used as an interim step are independent systems operators who have control, but not ownership, over the transmission in a particular region. This is an interim step I think, because there is a conflict between being an efficient generating company and an efficient transmission operator. Ultimately, whether it is 5 years from now or 10 years, we believe the transmission assets are going to be put into separate companies that cover very large areas and whose sole purpose is operating transmission systems, which will continue to be regulated businesses.

BILL: The trick is to make it desirable for someone to put investment into this transmission business. If there are no incentives, then it will not happen and you will see an awful lot of unreliability creep into our electric systems.

MARK: We think we will also see some very large distribution companies. If two or three companies sell off their generation, then these companies would want to get larger in order to achieve additional economies of scale. As a result, we may see some very large distribution companies likely offer additional services. For example, they may get into gas distribution and what Bill was talking about before: "behind the meter" services. They could offer heating, lighting, and air-conditioning services. In other words, a distribution company might come to a factory and say, "Instead of selling you kilowatt hours, we will keep your plant at 70 degrees. We will light your factory and if necessary we will make investments in your plant. Let us do it and we will charge a fixed rate and share with you the savings over what you paid last year."

STEVE: So they might update a factory's air-conditioning system, for instance?

BILL: They might update everything if necessary. There would be no burden of regulation on this type of arrangement.

MARK: And part of it could be going out and finding a cheaper supplier. Part of it could be putting in insulation or replacing inefficient motors. Also, these large distribution companies may start offering other services. Two examples are security systems and appliance repairs.

STEVE: ...To the individual homeowner?

MARK: Yes. People trust their local utility employees and are more comfortable with letting them into their homes.

STEVE: You are really talking about an expansion of the whole business model.

BILL: Of course.

MARK: The underlying growth of the basic electric utility business in this country is small. It has been growing at about $1^1/2\%$ annually. Total energy usage has actually been decreasing. Electric has been getting a bigger share and oil has been getting a smaller share of the energy pie. It is a mature industry.

STEVE: What you are describing is almost like a General Electric, which has its fingers in many different types of business pies. If that is the case, then these electric utilities will begin acting much like regular stocks.

BILL: That is where we are going!

STEVE: Earlier you mentioned reliability of service. The summer of 1998 featured several electric utilities running short on power. What went wrong and will electric service become more and more unreliable in the new age of deregulation?

MARK: We had some unusual circumstances. Let's talk about near term and long term. Near term, there were a number of nuclear plants that were out, and essentially that is what caused the problem. There also were failures by two small power marketers. Long term, everybody is relying on market forces to supply the power, and it is not going to be as reliable in the future as it was in the past.

BILL: Some people are going to be willing to pay extra for reliability. Those companies that can provide that reliability and really stand behind it with integrity will probably be able to sell power at a premium to certain customers.

MARK: Eight to ten years ago utilities were operating on the basis of a 15% reserve margin. In other words, they were engineered so that when operating at their peak they would still have 15% extra in case something went out. As they move toward competition, utilities have started reducing their targets from 15% to 10%. Unless they are paid to supply backup power, utility companies will likely continue to reduce reserve margins.

STEVE: What about returns going forward? What can be expected over the next 5 or 10 years for someone investing in the utilities sector?

BILL: We think that a 12% annual average is a very achievable return with a reasonably well-managed portfolio of utility stocks. I am talking about electric utilities. You might get more with selected gas utilities or telephone companies. Now with selected electric utilities there is a reasonable chance of getting price/earnings multiple expansion. So that 12% could be increased significantly with any significant multiple expansion. Currently, their earnings are priced at a large discount to the market.

MARK: Out of the last 20 years, we've only had five years with less than a 12% return. So 12% may be conservative.

BILL: If interest rates go lower, then utilities could do better. If they go higher, you tend to have a fairly quick dumping of the stocks. And then you regroup and go from there. Call it an opportunity.

MARK: And it is long-term rates that are important, not short-term.

BILL: Right, it's the 10-, 20-, and 30-year bond rates. If you look at the general equities market over the past five to eight years, the really successful portfolios have resulted from a heavy concentration in a rather small number of large-cap companies, particularly more recently. And those companies have experienced major multiple expansion on their shares. Now our stocks have not yet seen any significant multiple expansion. So among other things, that gives them an enhanced defensive position relative to the market at this particular time. When you couple that with the essential basic nature and relative stability of their businesses, which are electricity, gas, and telephone, their defensive position is enhanced further. Even if you have to do without something else, if it is 98 degrees, you are likely to have your air conditioning on. Another thing that adds to their defensive characteristic is that selected companies have very large net free cash flow. Big stock buybacks are just beginning. Our off-the-cuff estimate is that over the next couple of years you might see buybacks remove more than $30 billion in electric utility common stocks from the stock market. And that could have a tremendous positive effect on prices. Another thing is that American industry has benefited greatly from restructuring. Companies have been able to get their unit costs down. There has been a lot of consolidation. They have gotten lean and mean. And a significant part of that has already happened. But for our companies, this restructuring is just beginning. The reason it has not happened in the past is that they were too regulated. It really doesn't make much sense to cut everything to the bone if you have to give it all away in rate cuts. So they haven't done it. Some companies have enormous cost-cutting reservoirs ahead of them. As more and more of a company's business moves from being shackled and held down by the regulatory hand, you will see more of the benefits of what we have been talking about flow to its stockholders. These are very exciting times for selected companies. Electric and gas utilities are very much in a transition phase. What I would want any knowledgeable investor to understand is that from all of this are going to emerge some companies with great potential to put up some great numbers if you can just shake off the utility label. Yes, there will be increased volatility in the generation part of the business, but as compared with most other areas of the U.S. economy, it will still be low volatility.

STEVE: Then what percentage of that overall portfolio would you recommend be invested in utilities?

BILL: That depends on the type of person. Picture first a reasonably well-off retired couple. They have a pretty high standard of living. They own one or two homes and they have a good-size portfolio. To have as much as 25% in utilities is imminently practical. Someone young and developing may want to have far less in utilities. As an aside, I would say that the downside risk over the next few years is relatively small. Because even the poorly run companies will have a certain amount of value, owing to the likelihood that they will be acquired. However, one does not want to overstay in the weaker companies. It may be three or four years, but somewhere down the line those companies that are poorly managed will have their breakfasts taken away from them.

STEVE: Then is staying too long with these inept companies the greatest danger ahead or are there bigger pitfalls for the utilities investor?

MARK: That is an important question.

BILL: Regulation could raise its ugly head in any one state.

MARK: Interest rates are a key risk as well when investing in utility stocks. Because they are purchased for income, they remain interest rate sensitive. Also, about 60 percent of a utility's business continues to be regulated, so quality regulation is very important. In addition, most transition plans require legislation. Therefore, we need to consider the politics of the various state legislatures. Also, I mentioned earlier that many of these companies have gone from cash users to cash generators. In the 1980s many of them did stupid things with their money. They went into savings and loan and insurance industries among others. Fortunately now, they seem to be almost entirely in energy-related businesses. So another risk is that a utility would do something stupid. Related to this, and I wouldn't call it stupid, is that some utilities are investing overseas in some pretty risky countries. They could certainly get caught by surprise, and I think a number of them are going to be reevaluating their overseas strategies. Our fund is invested only in American utilities, although some of them have investments abroad....What I'm saying is that high international exposure is a risk. It could turn out to be good or bad, but it is a risk.

STEVE: Any other last words of warning or advice before I let you go?

MARK: The only other thing that I would say is that if dividend yields look too good, they usually are. You have to watch out for high payout ratios and yields that are well above the industry average, because that could be a signal that the company may be getting ready to cut the dividend.

BILL: The idea I would stress is that the potential for being rewarded, if you are smart about investing in these utility common stocks, is very, very good. And it can be way above market averages with lower risk. The great companies are putting down the platforms that will enable them to succeed. Already, it is pretty clear who some of the early winners are going to be. So I think that one should not underestimate the reward for doing a good job of investing in this area.

STEVE: All right. I thank you both for your time.

CHAPTER 10

Digging for Pay Dirt: Investing in Energy, Hard Assets, and Other Natural Resources

Why would you (or anyone else) invest in natural resources? No sector has been so beaten up, so depressed, and so disappointing to its diehard investors so many times. The gold bug was not-so-literally squashed in 1998 when gold fell below $275 an ounce; oil prices in 1998 (adjusted for inflation) hit their lowest level since 1972; and the major stock indexes of Western nations rich in natural resources—Canada, Australia, and New Zealand—have stagnated.

Fool's Gold

Natural resource open-end mutual funds have also performed poorly—averaging 3.8% annually for 5 years (1994–1998) and 7.1% for 10 years (1989–1998). The natural resource funds that avoid precious metals—for example, Price New Era, with a 10-year gain of 9.2%—have done best, while the pure gold funds have been pure money losers for mutual fund prospectors. One fund, U.S. Global Gold, lost 81.5% of its value in 10 years—a dismal 17.1% annual loss that easily clinched its infamous position as the absolute worst mutual fund from 1989 to 1998.

We see little hope for gold. It peaked at $800 an ounce in 1980, hovered mostly between $350 and $400 from 1995 to 1997, then fell to less than $275 by the summer of 1998, before ending the year near $290. Gold is both beautiful and ageless. Given its indestructibility and age-old history as a store of value, it's estimated that at least 98% of all the gold ever produced still exists today in one form or another. Thus, overall supply continually increases, adding to the likelihood that gold prices will remained depressed.

Mercantilism, now totally discredited, was the most popular and accepted economic theory from the 1500s to the 1700s. It claimed that the primary economic goal of each nation should be to accumulate gold by importing as much as possible while exporting as little as possible to achieve a favorable balance of trade. Adam Smith debunked mercantilism in his classic *Wealth of Nations,* written in 1776, by countering that accumulating gold did not necessarily make a nation wealthy. The real "wealth of nations," Smith argued, came from rising living standards promoted best by capitalistic exchange of goods and services within and between countries. However, old habits die hard as gold remained the primary way to settle trade imbalances between nations well into the twentieth century.

If You Must Invest

If you believe gold prices are going up, then buying gold or gold coins is not the way to make money. Buying gold companies is. For example, let's say gold mining company XYZ can produce gold for $290 an ounce. If gold sells for $300 an ounce, the company makes a $10 profit; however, if gold spikes to $330 an ounce, the company makes $40 an ounce. Thus, a 10% rise in gold prices from $300 to $330 an ounce produces a 300% gain in the gold mining company's profits. And when gold prices fall, as

> The shock of the Great Depression of the 1930s forced the United States and its major trading partners to outlaw trading and holding of gold by private companies and citizens; it wasn't until four decades later, in the 1970s, that U.S. citizens could legally buy and hold gold.

they have done consistently for the last five years, that same leverage can turn a profitable mining company into a huge money loser.

All companies that produce natural resources (not just gold) are subject to some degree to the same leverage—rising prices of the resource can produce magnified profit gains and falling prices can cause big losses and even bankruptcy. Producers have been able to offset some of their potential losses from falling raw material prices by technological breakthroughs that cut costs and through diversification—either by expanding into more control over processing and final retail sales or by extraction and production of other natural resources.

Oil

No companies dependent on natural resources have been more successful at coping with falling prices than the large oil producers. Given their success and the absolute dependence of all modern economies on their product, we believe that the best sector investment opportunities are in buying either energy-focused mutual funds or at least one of the major oil companies.

Certainly a higher-risk approach is owning one of the three major diversified oil services companies—Baker Hughes (BHI), Halliburton (HAL), or Schlumberger (SLB)—or purchasing the Fidelity Select Energy Service fund (FSESX; 3% load). The most volatile and the most depressed oil sector stocks at the end of 1998 were the drilling companies: the four big drillers are Diamond Offshore (DO), Global Marine (GLM), Rowan Cos. (RDC), and Transocean Offshore (RIG).

Crude oil prices peaked at $23 a barrel in November 1997, before falling more than 50% to less than $11 in 1998, finishing the year at $12.05. (Oil is shipped via oil tankers, pipelines, and trucks, but a barrel—42 gallons—is the measuring unit.) As oil prices plummeted, the leading producers—Exxon-Mobil, Royal Dutch Shell, and others—responded by cutting their budgets, forming partnerships, and even consolidating. This led to contracting for less business from the oil service and oil drilling companies. In the oil sector, when the majors sneeze their suppliers catch pneumonia. Two such sneezes came in late 1998 in when BP bought Amoco and Exxon and Mobil announced the biggest merger ever. The two new combined companies will not spend nearly as much money with suppliers as the original four companies would have if they had remained independent.

Basic Investing

For most beginning investors in the energy sector we recommend buying one of the oil giants and gradually buying more shares over several years. Four of them—BP-Amoco, Chevron, Exxon-Mobil, and Texaco—can be purchased directly; Exxon-Mobil even permits IRA purchases in its DRIP.

Another basic approach is to buy a diversified mutual fund. The lowest-risk no-commission way to invest in this sector is to buy the no-load Vanguard Energy Fund. Slightly less volatile is the Petroleum and Resources closed-end fund, managed by our expert for this chapter, Douglas Ober. This is an excellent buy-and-hold fund, particularly when it sells at a 10% discount or more. By far the highest-risk fund play is Fidelity Select Energy Service. (See Table 10-1.)

Oil Services

Obviously, for more experienced and very aggressive investors, the hot buy/sell action is in the oil services subsector. Beware, it's easy to get burned! From its peak in November 1997 to its bottom in October 1998, the Philadelphia oil service sector index of 15 industry leaders fell 65%. The number 1 oil service blue chip, Schlumberger, fell from a peak of $94.43 in late 1997 to a low of $40.06 in 1998. Every one of the other six major oil service and oil drilling stocks did even worse!

TABLE 10-1   Energy Fund Comparison

Fund	Standard Deviation	Beta	Annual Percentage Return				
			1994	1995	1996	1997	1998
Vanguard Energy	24.73	0.82	−1.6	+25.3	+34.0	+14.9	−20.5
Petroleum and Resources	20.87	0.82	−2.1	+27.0	+25.6	+18.8	−11. 1
Fidelity Select Energy Service	48.14	1.17	+0.8	+40.9	+49.0	+51.9	−49.7

Data source: Morningstar, Inc.

Yet, by late 1998, insiders were buying four times as many shares as they were selling of their own oil service stocks. According to Richard Cuneo, editor of the newsletter *Vicker's Weekly Insider Report,* a more normal ratio is 2 to 2.5 times as much *selling* as buying. Because of stock options given to key company personnel, insiders typically sell far more than they buy. Obviously, those who know their companies best see their stocks as bargains. Some insiders argue that, in addition to rock-bottom oil prices, their stocks are poised to move higher because the warm winters caused by El Niño are over, oil-producing countries are cutting back, and growth in world demand, while slowing, is still increasing.

For the oil service stocks to stage a sustained rally, oil prices will probably have to reach at least $16 a barrel and stay near or above that price for several months. However, Ken Miller, senior principal with the Houston-based oil consulting firm Purvin and Getz, claims that 1998's average production of 75.5 million barrels a day is too high. (OPEC countries supply about 40% of the total: 30.8 million barrels daily.) Miller believes that for the next few years there won't be enough demand to support production. As a result, he predicts that prices will hover around $15 a barrel until Asia works its way out of its slump.

Why Invest

We think the energy sector should be represented in every investor's portfolio. Compared with the broader market, it's quite cheap and it offers excellent diversification benefits. When the rest of your portfolio zigs, your energy investments often zag. We are also impressed by the ability of the oil majors to make good profits when gasoline was below $1 a gallon. How much will they make the next time oil prices skyrocket? And, given the indisputable law of supply and demand, there will be a next time!

Expert Interview

Of the seven experts interviewed in this book, only Douglas Ober is a closed-end mutual fund manager. This affords him the opportunity to remain oblivious to inflows or outflows of cash. Thus he can be more focused on picking natural resource stocks. He has done his job exceptionally well over the years and shares his knowledge with us here.

Douglas G. Ober is the chairman and chief executive officer of two closed-end funds, the Adams Express Co. and Petroleum and Resources Corp., with combined assets in excess of $2 billion. Douglas joined the firms in 1980 as a research analyst, became a member of the portfolio management team in 1986, and was elected chairman of the companies in 1991. He received his BS in engineering from Princeton University and a master's in finance from Loyola College in Baltimore, MD. He is also a chartered financial analyst.

STEVE: In what areas of the energy sector does your fund invest?

DOUGLAS: We invest in all segments of the oil and gas industry, from the integrated multinationals to the domestics to the small independent producers of oil and gas. We invest in refiners, drillers, service providers, gas pipeline and local distribution companies—all of that within the oil and gas environment. We also invest in basic materials. This includes companies that specialize in nonferrous metals, mining, precious metals, construction materials, and paper and forest products.

STEVE: How have you seen your area evolve over the past decade? Have you seen many changes in the natural resource and energy industry?

DOUGLAS: We see constant change. In the oil and gas industry, there are political factions that have tremendous effects on what's going on, particularly in the Middle East. You've got Iraq, a potential large producer of oil, severely limited at this point. Russia, which at one time was exporting more than 12 million barrels of oil a day, is now reduced. I think the Russians now export about 4 million barrels of oil a day. They produce 6 million and they export 4 million. Because there has not been any investment in the infrastructure, they could not produce 12 million barrels a day if they had to.

STEVE: There's just no capacity?

DOUGLAS: There's no capacity because they haven't had the capital to put into their facilities. So you've got the political situation. You've also got environmental considerations going on where if somebody wanted to build a new oil refinery in the United States today, it would be impossible.

STEVE: Because of all the regulations?

DOUGLAS: Yes. In terms of other structural changes, we've got these megamergers which have gone on and are likely to continue. British

Petroleum just bought Amoco. There is a conference going on in Vienna this week [October 1998] among the top 20 to 25 CEOs of multinational oil companies just to talk about what the future of the industry is.

STEVE: So do you see these kinds of changes continuing?

DOUGLAS: I think there will be some more mergers. There have been some incredibly successful joint ventures. We had one where Texaco merged their European refining and marketing assets, and that has been a very successful activity. There are a number of other companies that have the potential to make similar moves. You could see refining and marketing joint ventures in this country which would affect the whole balance of what's going on in the industry.

STEVE: Is that the only way to increase profits? With all the new drilling techniques, there seems to be a glut of oil. How are these producers going to continue to make a profit—simply by merging?

DOUGLAS: No, there are a lot of different ways to do it. The efforts toward joint venture and/or merging of some of the assets of these companies are primarily aimed at reducing refining capacity around the world. The European venture that I mentioned was principally designed to close a couple of refineries because there was too much refining capacity on the European mainland.

STEVE: So there is an effort by the oil companies to reduce the supply?

DOUGLAS: Yes, but not the supply of oil—rather, the capacity to refine the oil into gasoline, because there has been too much gasoline in Europe. Look at the price of gasoline in Europe compared with the price of gasoline in this country and you scratch your head and say, "What is going on here?" Because they pay three and four times what we pay for a gallon of gas. But for the demand in Europe, they have got too much capacity.

STEVE: Then prices should be falling in Europe as well.

DOUGLAS: They should be, but they are not.

STEVE: Why is that?

DOUGLAS: Primarily because the infrastructure in Europe is such that you cannot move the oil and gasoline from one country to another without incurring this, that, and the other tax, and all kinds of fees. Now with the change on continental Europe into the single monetary unit, the tearing down of borders, and so on, you may see changes there that will have significant effect on gasoline prices.

European governments typically level gasoline taxes of $2 a gallon or higher—a primary reason that most Europeans drive small cars.

STEVE: What about alternative fuel sources? Is that a significant threat to oil prices?

DOUGLAS: We don't see anything coming along that could significantly impact oil. At one time, people thought that nuclear fuel would solve everybody's problems. There have been tremendous strides made in solar power and that has been modestly successful. But there still need to be a few more leaps in solar power before it will be able to provide electricity for even small towns. So we don't see that as having a major impact. We do subscribe to some degree to the Club of Rome's thinking as far as what happens in the year—oh, it's probably 2030. [In the 1970s, the Club of Rome was predicting a severe oil shortage by 2000 to 2010.]

STEVE: What happens in 2030?

DOUGLAS: Oil just starts to run out.

STEVE: Even with the advanced drilling techniques?

DOUGLAS: Even with all of the advanced drilling techniques and everything else that we have been doing, the finds in the Caspian Sea and everything else, we are running out of oil. And it is out in that 2030 time frame that oil starts to run out, and we revert to back to a coal-based global energy economy.

STEVE: So then, that would seem to bode well for oil producers.

DOUGLAS: Well that's our feeling, for the long term.

STEVE: ...The very long term.

DOUGLAS: ...And even if it you look at a much shorter term. Yes, we have severe problems in Asia right now as well as other parts of the Far East, and that is reverberating throughout Latin America. But the simple fact is that two-thirds of the world's population consumes less than a quart of oil per capita per day. In the United States, we consume 11 quarts of oil per day per capita. So if that two-thirds of the world brings it up to just a quart a day, then that is a huge increase in the demand for oil. Which, again, bodes well for the oil and gas industry. And even though we are seeing a slackening in demand growth, demand is still growing worldwide. Demand has not flattened out and fallen off. It is growing at about 1% now, whereas it was growing at about 2% over the last four or five or six years with the tremendous growth in the Southeast Asian economies. But they are not the principal users. They are, on the margins, the biggest growers. But they are not, by any stretch of the imagination, the biggest users. So the Asian troubles have dampened demand for oil in what we refer to as the short term—being the next couple of years.

STEVE: What about the longer term? What kinds of returns can reasonably be expected in the energy sector over the next 5 to 10 years?

DOUGLAS: I believe that we will see returns that will be pretty close to the broader market returns. And there is a possibility that they could be significantly better.

STEVE: What have returns been like in the past?

DOUGLAS: If you go back and look at the numbers for the 10-year period ending in 1997, the S&P 500 returned something like 18%. For our fund, Petroleum and Resources Corp., it has been around 14%. So that's about a 4% differential. According to Morningstar, all equity funds have returned about 14% in those same 10 years. Growth and income funds: 15.2%. The 13 natural resource funds (other than Petroleum and Resources) tracked by Morningstar have had an 11% return over that 10-year period. So we think we are doing pretty well. We are taking on less risk and providing a better return to shareholders.

STEVE: Low risk with good returns—that's every investor's dream. Share your secrets. What are your buy criteria and how do you value a particular stock?

DOUGLAS: Focusing first on the oil and gas business—we look at a number of different characteristics. We look at the basic reserves that a company has. We look at their production wells and what it costs them to produce a barrel of oil. We look at cash flow. We want to know what their exploration activity is and where it is. If they are exploring in West Africa, that is a higher-risk operation than exploring in the Caribbean. We look at the amount of leverage that is incurred, what the regulatory environment is, and what the competition is. And since we are investing for the long term, the average turnover in our portfolio is approximately seven years. That is about a 16% turnover rate. So we are looking very hard at the management of the companies and what they're doing.

STEVE: Well, if you are going to hold a company for seven years, then you would definitely want to have a certain degree of confidence before you buy.

DOUGLAS: Our analysts go and visit with the companies and spend time with the management—not with just the IR [investor relations] people, but with the CEO, the chief financial officer, the operating people, and production. We are really interested in getting to know who the management is, what their strategies are, and how they operate. And as much as anything else, we want to know how adaptable they are, particularly in the oil and gas business. It is an environment that is constantly shifting. A year ago, you had oil at $23 a barrel and people were making money hand over fist. This year [1998] it got down to $11.

STEVE: How are they making money?

DOUGLAS: You have got to be flexible. You've got to know when to cut costs, when to cut your capital spending program, and how to react to these kinds of things—because oil is a volatile commodity. When you have a period where oil prices have fallen through the floor, you can't just shut everything down and say, "I'm not producing in this environment. I'm not going to do any more exploration in this environment." You would be cutting off your nose to spite your face. It is a short-term situation. The price of oil will not move back to $23 a barrel next year, but there is a limited supply of oil in the world. It will gradually move up in price. And so you have to think longer term.

STEVE: Are there other compelling reasons to invest in natural resources that we have yet to cover?

DOUGLAS: I think that a very significant reason is that, in general, the business is not as subject to the same domestic economic cycles as many other industries are. So you do not have that normal business cycle in the United States affecting your operations as it does many other companies. Whether they are steel companies or any others, they tend to be more U.S.-oriented than the multinational oil producers.

STEVE: So you get a lower correlation with other stock investments?

DOUGLAS: You get a lower correlation and therefore it serves as a counterbalance.

STEVE: Any other reasons to invest in natural resources?

DOUGLAS: In general, the oil companies have provided pretty substantial income returns in the form of dividends and that is certainly true today. And it is one of the few areas that does at this point.

STEVE: What about the dangers and pitfalls of investing in other natural resources? We all know what has happened to gold in recent years.

DOUGLAS: They are commodities. They are subject to short-term supply and demand swings. We talked about oil: it has gone from $23 a barrel down to $13, back up to $15 and now it is back down to the $11 range. If you look at copper, if you look at gold, if you look at any one of those commodities, they've got similar kinds of fluctuations. Still, one of the significant dangers is Russia. Russia used to be the largest producer of nickel in the world. They have not invested in infrastructure recently and their production of nickel has fallen off, but other producers have taken their place. About 70% of nickel goes into stainless steel and stainless steel use, particularly for buildings. And its use has fallen off. So there is a huge glut of nickel right now.

STEVE: And if Russia moves back into the market in a big way?

DOUGLAS: Russia needs dollars or some kind of export to generate foreign exchange. And that may include nickel, oil, and copper. Russia is a commodity-producing nation. They cannot sell a whole lot of those ugly old tractors. So they've got to go with commodities.

STEVE: And if they do, that would flood the market.

DOUGLAS: If they flood the market with commodities, then again, it would be tough for the Western companies to continue to produce at the rates that they do.

STEVE: What is the outlook, then, going forward for the harder assets?

DOUGLAS: For the precious metals, I don't see any significant improvement. With the world's level of inflation having come down as much as it has, the idea of gold being a storehouse of value just doesn't seem to hold water anymore. So people aren't hoarding it. I can't imagine a situation in which people would start hoarding gold again. So is it going to get back up to $800 an ounce [the all-time high in 1980]? I don't think so. A lot of the gold in this world had been held by the central banks in Europe. With the new EMU [European Monetary Union] and the decision as to how much gold is going to back the EMU, there is surplus gold in those central banks. They now have the opportunity to sell that off and several of them have.

STEVE: So when Warren Buffett bought large amounts of silver a while back, was that a mistake?

DOUGLAS: Silver is a little bit funnier game. There seem to be occasional new uses for silver that come out. Gold, with the exception of hoarding, jewelry, and some sophisticated electronics, doesn't seem to have much use. Furthermore, silver is a commodity that is not held in as many places. Central banks do not hold it, so there are not hordes of it that could be dumped on the markets if the price runs up. That's why back in the early 1980s the Hunt brothers were able to corner as much of the silver market as they did. That's why Buffett was able to accumulate a quarter of the world's current supply of silver. That's the character of that commodity.

STEVE: So the real key for these commodities—these precious metals—is whether or not some new use will be found for them such as in manufacturing, not simply the rush toward hoarding.

DOUGLAS: Exactly. Now with the commodity metals—copper, aluminum, and so on—the story is varied. Copper has a big infrastructure use. We use it for phone lines and for power lines, among other things. But the demand for copper has dropped off with the Southeast Asia difficulties because a lot of infrastructure building was happening in the islands of Southeast Asia, Thailand, and Malaysia, as well as in China. With the metals, you've got different situations that drive different metals. The palladium and platinum markets have been very good because the uses for them are in particularly exotic veins like exhaust converters. But copper is a very fundamental, basic unit of infrastructure.

STEVE: So then, given the above factors, how much should the investor have tucked away in the energy and precious metals sector?

DOUGLAS: I think that the exposure in general to the energy sector is light. Given the rather modest swings in the economy in recent years, we seem to have dampened down the economic cycle quite a lot. We don't have as much cyclical up and down in the economy, so perhaps one's need for that counterbalancing investment to the economy is low. But I think for investors who have any sort of need for income, in a relatively stable sort of operating situation, then the oils make good sense. The S&P weighting for energy is around $7^1/2\%$ and I think it is appropriate to have as much as 10% in energy. But then again, that depends somewhat on an individual's situation. If you are 25 years old, you do not need income coming in from your investments. Still, there are significant opportunities for capital gains based on what we see happening over the next 20 years or so. But you are not going to have a technology rocket here. It is a relatively stable industry dealing in a somewhat volatile commodity.

STEVE: Finally, of all the fund managers we interviewed, you run the only closed-end fund. Take a minute and explain the benefits of investing in a closed-end fund.

DOUGLAS: Closed-end managers have what I consider a very unique opportunity to take a long-term perspective on investing. We don't have funds coming in to be invested. We don't have redemptions and money being pulled out of the fund. If we decide to put $10 million or $10,000 in Exxon today, we are not going to have to sell some of that tomorrow because someone has redeemed some shares. We are able to invest in individual companies that may not be as liquid as private investors would desire if they were investing directly in that company. If an open-end fund were forced to liquidate a company like Apache Petroleum, and it had to sell 150,000 shares of Apache, it would take the fund a week and a half and the price would be half of what it was. We have the luxury of not having to do that. So we can focus best on the long term because we are not subject to those fluctuations. The other great opportunity for investors is that when they buy a closed-end fund, they are generally buying it at a discount to net asset value. Last time I looked, more than 70% of closed-end funds were trading at a discount. So if investors put $10,000 into Petroleum and Resources, and it is selling at a 10% discount, then they are getting the benefits of an $11,000 investment—10% more than what they put in. So while Exxon is yielding 2%, their effective yield is 2.2%. Obviously, there is a downside in that the discount could get wider. But that is a fluctuation investors could choose to play if they so desired.

STEVE: Thank you for your time. It has been very informative.

Putting It All Together

Sailing the Investment Sea: A Step-by-Step Approach to Getting Started

You're hooked! You faithfully read every word of our first 10 chapters. You are eager to test the sector ocean by wading in, feet first, with your eyes wide open. Perhaps even before you bought our book, you knew you were willing to risk a shipwreck or two on your own sector voyage. Or most likely, you've already had experience staying afloat as a sector investor and are looking to batten the hatches a little tighter before the next stock market storm strikes with unexpected fury.

Whatever. You certainly deserve our best practical advice to help get your investment boat shipshape so you can chart your course to those two famous islands: fame and fortune. We exaggerate: fame is not our game; you're on your own there. Our task is simpler: it's all about finding fortune—making you rich!

Start Early

We can "guarantee" wealth by retirement age to any Generation X'er (born from 1965 to 1979) who has a "middle class" or better income, saves at least 10% annually, and is willing to let a diversified stock portfolio grow for three decades or more. Yes, we do mean guarantee (albeit, somewhat conditionally). Our guarantee is based on two caveats: (1) the stock market must yield at least double-digit returns, as it has for the entire twentieth century, and (2) your skill as an investor must net you at least the average return for large-company U.S. stocks.

Unless you're lucky enough to inherit a fortune, or fortunate enough to have a job that pays the big salaries of athletes or movie stars, building wealth is exceedingly long term, but fairly easy. At the 12% annual stock return since 1945, an investment doubles in 6 years. A double every 6 years is certainly not bad if you let your money grow for 30 years: at 12% every $2,000 socked away today equals about $64,000 in three decades.

Defer or Avoid Taxes

We can never overemphasize the importance of deferring or avoiding taxes as you rig your portfolio for that long cruise to Fortune Island. Never let the federal and state governments collect taxes you can legally avoid or defer! *In other words, maximize your tax shelters!* Our tax reduction approach is a fairly simple three-step process:

1. *Always* invest enough money in your 401(k) or other pension plan at work to get any matching money offered by your employer. It's financial insanity to turn down free money!

2. Put $2,000 a year into the Roth IRA. Or consider a tax-deductible IRA if you need the tax rebate and meet the lower-income guidelines.

Since 1871, as the United States changed from a predominately agrarian society to an industrial one, the average large-company U.S. stock has returned more than 9% compounded. For the last seven decades plus, since 1926, the return has been almost 11%, and since World War II (1946–1998) it's been better than 12%. As Jeremy Siegel demonstrates in his best-seller *Stocks for the Long Run* (McGraw-Hill, 1998), $1 invested in the average U.S. stock in 1802 (when the New York Stock Exchange began) grew—in less than two centuries—to $7,470,000 by the end of 1997.

3. If you can afford it, max out your pension plan at work. U.S. law permits up to $10,000 for 401(k) plans; even though there's no employer match, you will still defer all federal and state income taxes.

We constantly meet clients with tens of thousands of dollars in stocks or other long-term savings who aren't taking full advantage of their tax shelters. We aren't sure whether it's ignorance, weird behavior, or excessive patriotism. Why pay more taxes than necessary?

Just about everyone knows about 401(k)s. However, there are three other pension plans available to all self-employed people and most small businesses: (1) Keoghs, (2) SEP-IRAs, and (3) simple IRAs. Also, if you work for a nonprofit organization (as a minister, teacher, government employee, etc.), you are eligible for a 403(b), and some government employees are eligible for 457 deferred compensation plans. The maximum annual contributions for pension plans are listed in Table 11-1.

Reduce Investment Costs

Be cost-conscious by paying attention to fees. High commissions and/or mutual fund expense ratios can tempest-toss your investment boat. Web trading, DRIPs, and no-load mutual funds with low expense ratios are ideal ways to accumulate wealth for the do-it-yourselfer. Every dollar saved in fees is an extra dollar that can grow exponentially for years and years.

TABLE 11-1   Deferral Limits for Various Retirement Plans

Plan Type	Dollar Limit	Percentage Limit
Simple IRA	$6,000 (employee)	None
401(k)	$10,000 (employee)	25%
403(b)	$10,000 (employee)	17%
457	$8,000 (employee)	25%
SEP IRA	$25,000 (employer)	15% (corporations), 13.04% (noncorporations)
Keogh (pension-purchase and profit-sharing plans)	$30,000 (employer)	20%

Use Dollar Cost Averaging

Stock volatility can act like an enemy submarine ready to destroy or damage your portfolio. However, you can avoid that sub's most deadly torpedoes by diversifying widely and using dollar cost averaging (DCA). By investing small amounts of money on a regular basis you buy fewer shares when the market peaks and more shares when it plunges. In a rising market—and the broad U.S. market always rises eventually—DCA lowers your average cost per share. In other words, the rougher the investment seas, the more money you make if you keep your boat afloat by investing regularly when most others are selling.

So there you have it. Pretty simple. (1) Start investing in stocks at an early age, (2) max out your tax shelters, (3) keep investment costs low, and (4) use dollar cost averaging to invest every month or quarter for three decades or longer. Follow those four steps and given the double-digit returns of U.S. stocks for more than seven decades (including the 89% market decline from September 1929 to July 1932) and the magic growth provided by compounding, you will be quite wealthy when you reach retirement age. We guarantee it!

Create a Portfolio

Creating a portfolio is exceptionally individualistic. If you are, or plan to be, a serious sector investor, you may want to buy your broadly diversified mutual funds through your pension plan at work. Most 401(k)s and other pension plans do not offer sector choices unless it's the stock of the com-

---

Let's say you invest $167 monthly ($2000/year) in a high-beta technology fund IRA that only matches a disappointing broader market average of 6% for the next 15 years. (We believe there's about 1 chance in a 100 that the market will average 6% or less for the next 15 years!) However, your supercautious friend invests $167 monthly in a CD IRA paying 6% for the next 15 years. Typically, depending on how jagged its peaks and valleys, your DCA into a technology mutual fund would net you 25% to 50% *more* than your friend's cautious investment—even though each of you earned the exact same average of 6% a year for 15 years. (Of course, your cautious friend may have worried a lot less!)

pany you work for. No matter how much you love your employer's prospects, individual stocks can and do go straight down. Suppose you invest heavily in your employer's stock and your company goes bankrupt. Not only do you lose your pension money; you are unemployed as well! We typically recommend that no more than 25% of your pension be invested in your employer's stock. If you work for a blue-chip company and have exceptional job skills, up to 50% may be acceptable, but only for very high-risk investors.

Perhaps the best way to be a sector investor is to broadly diversify at least 50% of your stock portfolio. Then put about 20% into good businesses located outside the United States (actually an asset allocation move rather than a pure sector play), and invest 10% into each of your three favorite sectors. Of course, if you are willing to diversify by buying all seven sectors that we review in this book—even the out-of-favor real estate and energy sectors—you may want your targeted sectors to be as high as 60% of your equity holdings.

Let's allocate a mythical portfolio that now totals $100,000. Jane Sample has $50,000 in a 401(k) at work and $50,000 in IRAs and other individually controlled money accounts that she wants to invest in her sector picks. Her 401(k) gives her an international fund choice (more than 60% of all employers now offer a 401(k) foreign fund option), but it does not have sector or employer stock choices available. We present both aggressive and moderate models in Tables 11-2 and 11-3.

The following sector possibilities are in alphabetical order. Our individual stock selections are mostly blue chip and are based on market conditions at the end of 1998. These potential picks are obviously frozen in time. While we have attempted to offer great long-term choices, circumstances change and the individual investor must do some homework before investing. (For many of the closed-end funds, we list the minimum discount target for purchase consideration.)

TABLE 11-2   Jane's 401(k): $50,000

Aggressive		Moderate	
Large-cap U.S. stock funds	$20,000	Large-cap U.S stock funds	$25,000
Small- to midcap stock funds	15,000	Small- to midcap stock funds	12,500
International stock funds	15,000	International stock funds	12,500

TABLE II-3   Jane's Sector Investments: $50,000 (IRAs and taxable accounts: hold funds in IRAs, stocks in taxable accounts whenever possible)

Aggressive		Moderate	
Technology stocks/funds	$15,000	Technology stocks/funds	$7,500
Health care stocks/funds	10,000	Health care stocks/funds	7,500
Financial stocks/funds	10,000	Financial stocks/funds	7,500
ADRs, area international and/or single-country funds	10,000	Diversified and/or area international funds	5,000
Energy stocks/funds	2,500	Energy stocks/funds	7,500
Utilities stocks/funds	2,500	Utilities stocks/funds	7,500
		Real estate stocks/funds	7,500

Technology and Communication

Stocks—**America Online, Bell South, Cisco Systems, Dell, GTE, Intel, Lucent, MCI Worldcom,** and **Microsoft**

No-loads—**Dreyfus Technology Growth, Firsthand Technology Value, Invesco Technology, Invesco Worldwide Communications, Janus Global Technology, Price Science and Technology,** and **Montgomery Global Communications**

Load funds—**Alliance Technology, Fidelity Select Computers, Fidelity Select Developing Communication,** and **Fidelity Select Electronics**

Closed-end—**Gabelli Global Media** (GGT, 15% discount)

Health Care

Stocks—**Abbott Labs, Amgen, Bristol-Myers Squibb, Merck,** and **Pfizer**

No-loads—**Firsthand Medical Specialists, Invesco Health, Janus Global Life Sciences, Vanguard Health Care** (closed to new investors), and **Warburg-Pincus Health Sciences**

Load funds—**Eaton Vance Health Sciences, Fidelity Select Biotech,** and **Fidelity Select Health**

Closed-end—**Invesco Global Health** (GHS, 12% discount)

Financial Services

Fund companies/brokerages—**E-Trade, Morgan Stanley Dean Witter, Schwab,** and **T. Rowe Price**

Banks—**BB&T, Bank One, Chase Manhattan, Citigroup, Mellon, Regions Financial,** and **Toronto Dominion**

Insurance companies—**All-State, American Insurance Group, Annuity and Life Re-Holdings,** and **Equitable**

No-loads—**FBR Small Cap Financial** and **Price Financial Services**

Load funds—**Fidelity Select Home Finance**

Closed-end—**John Hancock Bank and Thrift Opportunity** (BTO, 12% discount)

International

Stocks—**BP-Amoco, Daimler-Chrysler, Nokia,** and **Royal Dutch Shell**

Diversified no-loads—**American Century International Discovery, Artisan International, BT International Equity, Fidelity Diversified International, Harbor International Growth,** and **Vanguard International Growth**

Diversified load funds—**EuroPacific Growth** and **Putnam International Growth**

Closed-end—**Global Small Cap** (GSG, 20% discount)

EMERGING MARKETS

No-loads—**Fremont Emerging Markets** and **Managers Emerging Markets**

Load funds—**Nicholas-Applegate Emerging Markets** and **Templeton Developing Markets**

Closed-end—**Emerging Markets Telephone** (ETF, 20% discount)

AFRICA AND THE MIDDLE EAST

Load funds—**Calvert Africa**

Area closed-end—**F&C Middle East** (EMF), **Morgan-Stanley Africa** (AFF, 24% discount), and **Southern Africa** (SOA)

Single-country closed-end—**First Israel** (ISL, 24% discount)

ASIA

No-loads—**Price New Asia, Montgomery Emerging Asia, Warburg-Pincus Japan Growth,** and **Warburg-Pincus Japan Small Company**

Load funds—**Colonial Newport Tiger** and **Fidelity Japan Small Company**

Closed-end—**Morgan-Stanley Asia** (APF, 22% discount) and **Scudder New Asia** (NEF, 17% discount)

Single-country closed-end—**India** (IFN, 25% discount), **Singapore** (SGF), **Taiwan** (TWN, 22% discount), and **Templeton China** (CHN, 20% discount)

WEBS—**Hong Kong** (EWH), **Malaysia** (EWN), and **Japan** (EWJ)

AUSTRALIA AND NEW ZEALAND

No-load—**Capstone New Zealand**

Closed-end—**First Australia** (IAF, 24% discount)

WEBS—**Australia** (EWO)

CANADA

Stock—**Imax**

Load funds—**Fidelity Canada** and **Ivy Canada**

Closed-end—**Canadian World Limited** (CWF, 30% discount, on Toronto exchange)

WEBS on AMEX—**Canada** (EWC)

EUROPE

No-loads—**Price Europe, Scudder Greater Europe,** and **Vanguard European Index**

Load funds—**Fidelity European Capital Appreciation, Morgan-Stanley/Dean Witter Europe,** and **Putnam European Growth**

Area closed-end—**European Warrant Fund** (EWF, 20% discount) and **Scudder New Europe** (NEF, 20% discount)

Single-country closed-end—**Austria** (OST, 17% discount), **Irish Investment** (IRL, 15% discount), **Italy** (ITA), **France Growth** (FRF), **New Germany** (GF), **Spain** (SNF), **Turkish Investment** (TKF, 20% discount), and **United Kingdom** (UKM)

WEBS—**France** (EWK), **Germany** (EWG), **Italy** (EWI), **Netherlands** (EWN), **Spain** (EWP), **Sweden** (EWD), **Switzerland** (EWL), and **United Kingdom** (EWU)

LATIN AMERICA

No-loads—**Price Latin America** and **Scudder Latin America**

Load funds—**Fidelity Latin America**

Area closed-end—**Latin America Discovery** (LDF, 22% discount)

Single-country closed-end—**Argentina** (AF), **Brazil** (BZF, 25% discount), **Chile** (CF, 25% discount), and **Mexico Equity and Income** (MXE, 25% discount)

WEBS—**Mexico** (MXF)

Real Estate

Stocks—**Boston Properties, Duke Realty, Highwoods Properties, Host Marriott, Kilroy Realty,** and **Starwood Hotels and Resorts**

No-loads—**American Century Real Estate, CGM Realty, Fidelity Real Estate, Longleaf Partners Realty,** and **Vanguard REIT Index**

Load funds—**Alpine U.S. Real Estate, Davis Real Estate, Franklin Real Estate,** and **Templeton Global Real Estate**

Closed-end—**Cohen and Steers Realty Trust** (RFI, 10% discount)

Utilities

Stocks—**Ameren, Atmos Energy, Duke Energy, FPL Group,** and **Southern Co.**

No-loads—**American Century Utilities, Fidelity Utilities, Strong American Utilities,** and **Vanguard Utilities Income**

Load funds—**Fidelity Select Utilities Growth** and **MFS Utilities**

Closed-end—**Duff and Phelps Utility Income** (DNP)

Natural Resources (Emphasis on Energy)

Stocks—**Atwood Oceanics, Chevron, BP-Amoco, Exxon-Mobil, Haliburton, Noble Drilling, Schlumberger,** and **Texaco**

No-loads—**Invesco Energy, Price New Era, Robertson-Stephens Global Natural Resources,** and **Vanguard Energy**

Load funds—**Fidelity Select Energy** and **Fidelity Select Energy Services**

Closed-end—**Petroleum and Resources** (PEO, 15% discount)

Use the Internet

In Chapter 4, we heralded the potential of the Internet to inform and empower. But it can also save you money. So our best recommendation for getting started is to open up an online trading account.

Any serious sector investor must be Internet capable. Online trading is by far the least expensive way to invest. Professional analysis and recommendations of specific stocks are readily available. Morningstar data and screening capabilities for mutual funds can be found on the Net. In essence, professional help can be accessed for free. And there is so much more.

Table 11-4 presents a list of the best free Web sites on the Internet. Our personal favorite free Web site is Quicken.com. Individual portfolios can be set up by entering stock and fund symbols. These portfolios are updated automatically and, unlike the listings at many sites, they appear on the home page along with alerts about any new information on the individual securities. In further contrast to other free sites, Quicken uses Morningstar data to break down mutual fund holdings by investment category. But perhaps Quicken's most distinguishing characteristic is its colorful pie charts, which break down a portfolio according to market cap and asset class. It also compares your current positions against an ideal portfolio with an optimal risk/reward ratio.

TABLE II-4   The Best Free Web Sites

Site Name	Internet Address	Objective
1040.Com	www.1040.com	Tax information
AARP Investment Program	aarp.scudder.com	Mutual funds
ADR.com	www.adr.com	ADRs
ASK Research Stock Charting & Analysis	www.askresearch.com	Technical analysis
American Century	www.americancentury.com	Mutual funds
Bank Rate Monitor	www.bankrate.com	Mortgage calculator
Berger Funds	www.bergerfunds.com	Mutual funds
BigCharts	www.bigcharts.com	Stock charts and analysis
BigCharts Canada	canada.bigcharts.com	Foreign investing
Bonds Online	bondsonline.com	Bonds
CBS MarketWatch	cbs.marketwatch.com	Financial news
Chicago Board of Options Exchange	www.cboe.com	Options/futures
Chicago Board of Trade	www.cbot.com	Options/futures
Coffee, Sugar, and Cocoa Exchange	www.csce.com	Options/futures
CyberInvest.com	www.cyberinvest.com	Investment Web links
Daily Stocks	www.dailystocks.com	Stock/fund quotes
Depository Receipt Services	www.bankofny.com/adr	ADRs
Equis International	www.equis.com	Technical analysis
Equity Analytics	www.e-analytics.com	Stock data and analysis
Fidelity Investments	www.fidelity.com	Mutual funds
Financenter.com	www.financenter.com	Personal finance
Franklin Templeton and Mutual Series Funds	www.franklin-templeton.com	Mutual funds
Good Money	www.goodmoney.com	Social concerns
ICI Mutual Fund Connection	www.ici.org	Mutual funds

TABLE II-4   *(Continued)*

Site Name	Internet Address	Objective
INVESCO	www.invesco.com	Mutual funds
InfoFund	www.infofund.com	Portfolio tracking
Internal Revenue Service	www.irs.ustreas.gov	Tax information
Investor Square	www.investorquare.com	Mutual funds
Investor's Business Daily Web Edition	www.investors.com	Financial news and analysis
Ivestorama	www.investorama.com	Investment Web links
Janus	www.janus.com	Mutual funds
LifeNet	www.lifenet.com	Life insurance
MarketGuide	www.marketguide.com	Stock data
Microsoft Money Insider	moneyinsider.msn.com	Tax information
MoneyScope	www.moneyscope.com	Stock quotes
Moneypages	www.moneypages.com	Investment Web links
Montgomery Funds	www.montgomeryfunds.com	Mutual funds
Motley Fool	www.fool.com	Stock data and analysis
Mutual Fund Investor's Center	www.mfea.com	Mutual funds
Mutual Funds Interactive	www.fundsinteractive.com	Mutual funds
NASD Regulation Inc.	www.nasdr.com	Regulations
Nasdaq Stock Market	www.nasdaq.com	Stock exchange
Nueberger Berman	www.nbfunds.com	Mutual funds
Quicken Financial Network	www.qfn.com	Personal finance
Quicken.com	www.quicken.com	Stock/fund charts/tracking
Quotesmith Corporation	www.quotesmith.com	Life insurance
Royce Funds	www.roycefunds.com	Mutual funds
Safeco Funds	www.safecofunds.com	Mutual funds
Scudder Funds	www.scudder.com	Mutual funds

TABLE II-4   (*Continued*)

Site Name	Internet Address	Objective
SmallCap Investor	www.smallcapinvestor.com	IPOs
SteinRoe Funds	www.steinroe.com	Mutual funds
Strong Funds	www.strong-funds.com	Mutual funds
T. Rowe Price	www.troweprice.com	Mutual funds
U.S Bureau of Public Debt/Treasury Direct	www.publicdebt.treas.gov	Bonds
U.S. Securities and Exchange Commission	www.sec.com	Regulations
Vanguard	www.vanguard.com	Mutual funds
Wall Street City	www.wallstreetcity.com	Stock screening
Wall Street Research Net	www.wsrn.com	Investment Web links
William F. Sharpe's Home Page	www-sharpe.stanford.edu	Education

Data source: *AAII Journal,* September 1998.

The Quick Start

Let's summarize this chapter and give you a sample step-by-step approach to getting started. From our vantage point, the following steps are listed in order of importance for long-term sector investing.

1. Participate in an employer-sponsored retirement plan to the extent that the employer offers matching contributions. Put 50% in large-company stocks, 25% in mid/small-company stocks, and 25% in international stocks.

2. Open a Roth IRA account. (Waterhouse offers IRAs without custodial fees.) Put $2,000 into Janus Global Life Sciences or Warburg-Pincus Health Sciences Fund.

3. Go back to the employer-sponsored pension plan and defer the maximum amount allowable.

4. Open an account with T. Rowe Price and dollar-cost-average at least $50 a month through automatic checking account drafts first

into Price Science and Technology, then into Price Financial Services. (Other discount brokerages or mutual fund companies can be used, but T. Rowe Price is one of the few that allows you to start with as little as $50.)

5. Open an online brokerage account at a discount broker. As you save, buy the following in $2,500 chunks:

- Artisan International fund or Tweedy Browne Global Value fund
- Intel or Cisco Systems
- Merck or Pfizer
- FBR Small Cap Financial fund or John Hancock Bank and Thrift Opportunity fund
- Microsoft or Dell
- BB&T or T. Rowe Price
- Nokia or America Online
- Strong American Utilities fund or Duke Energy
- Exxon-Mobil or Petroleum and Resources fund

After completing all of the above, you should be well on you way to becoming an expert sector investor. The only thing left to do is check the sector weightings of your overall portfolio every few months to make sure you are hitting your target percentages for each sector. Stay focused. Stay informed. Stay disciplined. You will be successful.

12

Avoiding Rough Waters: Cautions and Conundrums for the Sector Investor

Y ou've read the book. You've picked out your favorite sectors, and now you have your strategies in place for making your small fortune in sector investing. You are thinking, "I am ready to 'set sail.' Let me just skim through these closing pages and I'm on my way." But hold on there, just one minute. Although we appreciate your enthusiasm for our book, we did have a reason for putting "Cautions and Conundrums" in the title of our last chapter.

Cautions

There is definitely money to be made in sector investing. No question about it: make the right decisions and "early retirement" pops into casual conversation more often than "How about the weather?" But there are two sides to the sector coin.

Let us illustrate. One of the best-performing mutual funds for the 10 years from October 1, 1988 to September 30, 1998 was Fidelity Select Health Care. A $10,000 investment would have netted $91,568 over that time period for a total return of 816%. We believe most people would find those returns more than acceptable. Conversely, that same $10,000 invested in the fund we highlighted in Chapter 10—U.S. Global Gold Shares—would have dwindled to $1,791 in those same 10 years. (See Table 12-1.) Many of you are undoubtedly thinking, "What kind of fool would invest in gold anyway?" But look at Table 12-2. Notice that Gold Shares vaults ahead of Select Health Care in the first 16 months. In fact, that October 1, 1988 purchase of Gold Shares would have just about doubled by early 1990; and again, most people would find that quick rise more than acceptable.

Now here's the caution for which you have been patiently reading. Momentum is intoxicating. Quick hits and fast money entice even the most seasoned investor. The temptation to ride "ole Mo" to the very top lures like cheese in a mousetrap. But when momentum shifts, the trap can chop off more than your tail if you don't get out quickly.

Finishing our gold example, let's suppose a would-be investor (we'll call him old Mr. Mo Mentum) saw the rise in Gold Shares and resolved to jump in on the first day of 1990. He put $100,000 into the fund, which was most of his retirement money. After all, gold is a

TABLE 12-1   The Tale of Two Sector Funds, October 1, 1988 to September 30, 1998

Fund	Total % Return	Value of $10,000 Initial Investment
Fidelity Select Health Care	816%	$91,568
U.S. Global Gold Shares	−82%	$1,791

Data source: Morningstar, Inc.

TABLE 12-2   The Tale of Two Sector Funds, October 1, 1988 to January 31, 1990

Fund	Total % Return	Value of $10,000 Initial Investment
Fidelity Select Health Care	33.9%	$13,389
U.S. Global Gold Shares	97.5%	$19,748

Data Source: Morningstar, Inc.

"safe" investment. Following a brief initial rise, Mr. Mo Mentum would have painfully watched his $100,000 become $55,480 just one year later, and $27,280 by the end of 1992. (Don't feel sad for old Mo. He's been well supported by Medicaid ever since.) Why did he hang on so long? Why didn't he just sell? Well, "It had a nice gain that first month" and "It's bound to come back" may have been part of his rationale. If only Mr. Mentum had chosen Fidelity Select Health Care.

Granted, we have chosen a rather extreme example. But the point is made. When everything looks rosy and a favored sector or fund has shot up for months or even years: *beware!* A hard, long fall is not impossible. You may be standing on a precipice enjoying the view. Just don't take another step.

Another caution for the sector investor comes when choosing a mutual fund. Some funds may be labeled as one type but have significant assets of a totally different type. For instance, some utilities funds have gotten a little tech heavy as they invest in telecom companies. Others, in search of more growth, have invested in financial stocks. So while someone might want the relative safety of utilities, it's possible to wake up one day and watch a utility fund take a sudden dip as techs and financials sell-off.

A related sector fund problem is overspecialization, or too much emphasis on subsectors. According to Morningstar, there were 134 sector funds in 1993. By 1999, that number more than doubled. Many of these new sector funds now concentrate on just one area of a broad sector. A financial fund may buy only small banks or a technology fund may buy primarily medical technology or biotech. So if investors are not careful, they could end up with a biotech fund when they thought they were getting a diversified technology fund. The answer is straightforward: do your homework.

Conundrums

A conundrum is a quandary; a problem for which there seems no solution; a catch-22 if you will. Unfortunately, sector investing has a few of them. The thoughtful reader may have even recognized a few conundrums throughout the preceding pages.

One puzzle comes from our experts. As dutiful students, we may want to follow each expert's advice to the letter. One question posed concerned the percentage that they would recommend be invested in their sector.

Table 12-3 shows the percentages that each of our experts suggested might be right for an investor's overall portfolio. The catch is that when added together, the total comes to 119.7%. And this does not even include sectors, such as transports, that we left out of this book. Short of leveraging, a portfolio cannot be more than 100% invested. So no matter how compelling the arguments are for each sector, choices must be made. Some sectors must be excluded, or at least significantly underweighted.

Why not just equally weight each sector? Or, say, use the weightings of the S&P 500 as a guide? This would avoid the above-described conundrum, right? Stop! Now go back and read the last three sentences again—out loud. Did you hear what you just read? This diversified approach would allow you to participate in each sector, but at the expense of the possibility of outperformance. You might as well just buy an index fund. So while we preach diversification as a way to lower risk, too much diversification relegates a portfolio to the annals of the average. No, the true sector investor must narrow his or her choices, roll the dice a bit, and passionately pray for decisions that are better than old Mr. Mo Mentum's.

TABLE 12-3   Expert Recommendations for the Percentage of Each Sector to Be Included in an Overall Portfolio

Sector	% Recommended
Technology	17.1%*
Financial	17.1%*
Health care	18%
International	22.5%
Real estate	10%
Utilities	25%
Natural resources	10%
Total	**119.7%**

*Represents an average of the other five sector recommendations, since these experts did not give a specific number.

The Psychology of Investing

Another conundrum comes from the human psyche. What causes people to invest too quickly—to "leap" before they "look"? Or why are some continually afraid to leap even after extensive looking? It's basic psychology. For many and varied reasons, our investment choices are based on far more than just rational thought. To paraphrase Ghandi, "The worst devils are in your own head."

RESEARCH TIP

For a better understanding of investing psychology, read *The Psychology of Smart Investing* by psychiatrist David Garfield (John Wiley & Sons, 1992).

Lack of action can be most fully explained by fear of regret. Consider recently deceased Uncle Joe. He left you $10,000 worth of a speculative Internet stock. And even though you are a sector investor, you would never gamble that much on such a volatile stock. You don't have that much risk tolerance. Still, a year after Uncle Joe's estate was settled, you find yourself hanging on to his stock. Why? Because we all have an innate desire to avoid feeling stupid. We humans kick ourselves much harder when we make dumb moves than when we fail to make smart ones. In other words, you would feel far worse if you sold Uncle Joe's Internet stock and it became the next Dell than if you did nothing and it became worthless.

This investor inertia can be found lounging around a portfolio as too many investors avoid selling a fallen stock until it gets back to even. Paralyzed by fear of regret, most hold on to losers far too long. Because it isn't until after the stock is sold that real money feels lost. And losing money inevitably feels twice as bad as making money feels good.

Inversely, many will act on investment ideas with little regard for the risk. They have no apparent fear as they gamble on hitting it big. The idea of winning on a really long shot proves so enticing that the odds are ignored and luck is trusted. This is, of course, good for state lotteries and internet IPOs, but bad for rational thought.

Another reason humans leap before looking is self-deluded overconfidence. In surveys, 80% of drivers say they are above average. Obviously that can't be. Only 50% are above average and 50% below. Add a few past stock successes to this natural overconfidence and a feeling of invincibility ensues as investment decisions become less well researched.

Nowhere is this phenomenon more apparent than when picking mutual funds. Many investors play the hot hand. The thinking goes that a number 1 fund last year will be the number 1 fund this year. And it may be. Or the manager may have been just plain lucky. Remember, sectors do rotate. The hot sector this year may be the cold one next year. Choosing a fund solely on percentage return is unfounded confidence.

So the lesson here is to "know thyself." Are you given to fear or greed? Do you tend toward quick action or endless inertia? Understand your nature. Then, override the irrational and invest with confidence, but not too much.

Lessons Gleaned

The final piece to the sector puzzle comes from listening and learning from the experts. Each of our gurus had much to say on his or her individual sector. But common principles and themes regularly surfaced. We offer just 10 here.

1. **Know what you own.** David Ellison refused to buy Bankers Trust because he could not understand for "more than an hour at a time" how it made money. Kevin Landis believes that when it comes to picking an individual tech stock, it depends on the "investor's background." The investor should know the company "pretty well" before investing.

2. **Management is key.** "Management is going to make a very big difference," says Mark Luftig of his utility sector. Mark Yockey and Andrew Davis concur. "You look for companies that have a logic…to how they are managed" and "You want great management in place with the companies you decide to work with" are their respective comments. And Pat Widner finds many different types of management skills to be "absolutely critical" in the health care industry. Finally, Douglas Ober is convinced that management must be "adaptable" and "flexible" in order to survive in the energy business.

3. **Sectors rotate.** From Pat Widner's perspective, it is impossible for health care to outperform "every year." "It runs in cycles," says Mark Yockey of international investments. And Andrew Davis needs "other believers" before his outcast real estate sector can rotate back to positive numbers.

4. **Avoid selling low.** Kevin Landis was particularly strong about selling low, stating that he believed the "number 1 risk" for investors in his tech sector was pulling out when the sector inevitably sold off. He goes on to say that selling out on the dips is "one of the few ways…of losing money in a growth industry." So he advised that we "assume the worst" when deciding how much money we could afford to tie up in technology long term. Pat Widner adds, "Hold on, and you will do fine."

5. **Be a long-term investor.** David Ellison maintains that the financial sector "is not your game" if you have a short-term time horizon. "You have to think longer term" can be no more true than it is for Douglas Ober's hamstrung oil sector. Pat Widner is adamant that "health care is a long-term investment."

6. **Sector investing depends on individual circumstances and risk tolerance.** "It depends on the type of person" (William Reaves), "It varies so much from case to case" (Kevin Landis), and "That depends somewhat on an individual's situation" (Douglas Ober) sample the thoughts of our experts on risk tolerance.

7. **Sector investing has its rewards.** "Health care will be a sector that outperforms the market" argues Pat Widner. According to William Reaves, returns can be "way above market averages," even for utilities.

8. **Timing the market is difficult.** Pat Widner says that health care's upside cannot be timed, because "no timing event acts as a catalyst."

9. **Think independently.** Mark Yockey urges us not to "follow the crowd" or "chase" hot investments.

10. **The future is more important than the past.** Andrew Davis feels "part of the market's beauty" is that it looks toward future earnings, not past.

And with that we close. Ultimately, it is the future for which we invest. Part of life's beauty is that we, as investors and as humans, look to the future, not the past. Learn from the past, but live, and invest, for the future. No one in the world's history has ever had the investment opportunities now available to you. May your future be truly profitable.

INDEX

ABOUT THE AUTHORS

Larry Hungerford, Ph.D., and **Steve Hungerford** are partners in the $75 million Woodard & Company Asset Management Group, Inc. They co-host the weekly television program *The Money Doctor*, and both also frequently appear on other broadcast programs to discuss investments. Dr. Hungerford, former director of a university center for economic education, is a popular lecturer on mutual funds and sector investing